On Thin Ice

On Thin Ice

AN EPIC FINAL QUEST INTO THE MELTING ARCTIC

ERIC LARSEN

WITH HUDSON LINDENBERGER

GUILFORD, CONNECTICUT

An imprint of Globe Pequot

Falcon and FalconGuides are registered trademarks of Rowman & Littlefield.

Distributed by NATIONAL BOOK NETWORK

800-462-6420

British Library Cataloguing-in-Publication Information available

The Library of Congress has cataloged the hardcover edition as follows:

Names: Larsen, Eric, 1971- author. | Lindenberger, Hudson, author.

Title: On thin ice : an epic final quest into the melting Arctic / Eric Larsen and Hudson Lindenberger.

Description: Guilford, Connecticut : Falcon, [2016]

Identifiers: LCCN 2016030256 (print) | LCCN 2016032249 (ebook) | ISBN 9781493022960 (hardcover) | ISBN 9781493022977 (ebook)

Subjects: LCSH: Larsen Eric, 1971- | Explorers—Arctic Regions—Biography.

Classification: LCC G635.L37 A3 2016 (print) | LCC G635.L37 (ebook) | DDC 910.911/3—dc23

LC record available at https://lccn.loc.gov/2016030256

ISBN 978-1-4930-3367-6 (paperback)

∞™ The paper used in this publication meets the minimum requirements of American National Standard for Information Sciences—Permanence of Paper for Printed Library Materials, ANSI/NISO Z39.48-1992.

CONTENTS

A Walking Buffet

Coordinates: 83.09 Degrees North, 474 Miles to North Pole

Sheer luck is the only reason I am here today to tell this story. I should be dead; a statistic. I should be a person whose name only gets mentioned on Wikipedia in the past tense. I should be the guy who got eaten by polar bears on his way to the North Pole, because I almost did.

Most people's first thought when they hear about the North Pole is based on childhood stories of Santa Claus. His workshop filled with elves making toys and his herd of flying reindeer. They think of solid, flat ground covered in snow. A nice place to go cross-country skiing. Well, let me tell you, that's not true. First off, there is no land north of the 84th parallel, which circles the Arctic Ocean just north of Greenland. There's only an endless expanse of sheet ice, continually in motion, breaking apart and bashing back together. It forms huge pressure ridges with ice rubble that can reach 20 feet tall and extend for miles, creating havoc for polar explorers. Secondly, the not-always-solid ice sits over the 14,000-foot-deep Arctic Ocean that, while affected by global warming, still registers at 29 degrees Fahrenheit and can mean a quick death for anyone falling through. Lastly, the polar bears that roam the pack ice hunting seals are hungry. The rare humans who venture into their domain often turn into a meal.

My expedition partner, Ryan Waters, and I had been struggling across the fractured, frozen moonscape, continually feeling our way through, around, and over the obstacles in our way. After five days on the ice, we had advanced a paltry 6.8 miles and still could see the relatively low mountains of Ellesmere Island,[1] our starting point, looming behind us.

Left: Polar Bear Tracks

Frustration was mounting quickly. Ryan is a veteran mountain guide with of over three dozen ascents of some of the tallest mountains in the world under his belt. He is a big guy at six-foot-two, with bushy black hair and an easygoing nature. I knew I would need his levelheadedness to help off-set my more aggressive nature if we were going to succeed.

If we had not been pushing, pulling, and lifting our two 317-pound sleds every step of the way, the beauty of our surroundings would have been overwhelming. Massive blocks of blue aquamarine ice towered above us, crazily tilted at all angles. Climbing the rubble piles reminded me of ascending the frozen hills of my youth in Wisconsin. The windswept snowfields between each pressure ridge contained an infinite collection of natural runnels, chutes, and shimmering crystals.

Believe it or not, I really don't like being cold, and therefore I work diligently to keep the cold as far away as possible.

All I could focus on was the need to keep moving north, increase our speed, and not freeze. The air surrounding us is a balmy -30 degrees—that's 10 degrees warmer than yesterday—and I am wrapped in layers upon layers of clothing and gear to keep it at bay.

Believe it or not, I really don't like being cold, and therefore I work diligently to keep the cold as far away as possible. Here, any exposed skin can start to show signs of frostbite within a few minutes in these temps. No part of my body is exposed, and my head is swathed in multiple layers of balaclava, hat, and neck gaiter, hidden from view by the thick fur ruffle of my coat's hood, wrapped tightly around my goggles. The large home-made nose beak protruding from my goggles acting as a final windbreak. Each breath I inhale is bitter cold but crisp and clean. It has a taste to it. A flavor I know all too well.

Thanks to the pressure ridges, we were forced to ferry each of our two sleds forward together, working as a team. We had hoped to each be pull-ing our own sled by this time, but that was not to be. The ice was too bad. Much like the teams of dogs I used to use back home, the two of us are harnessed to one sled. I am in the lead, with Ryan three feet behind me as we drag it over the ice and snow. We would move one sled as far forward as we feasibly could before unhooking and heading back to bring the next sled up. The work was mind-numbing and exhausting but required complete focus to make sure we didn't slip off a ridge, fall off a block, or get crushed by the heavy sled from behind. With the wind roaring down off the mountains at our backs, driving sheets of snow

The terror was immediate.

by us, plus clouds continually passing in front of the sun, on top of our field of vision being confined by our goggles, visibility could shrink to a few feet within a matter of minutes.

It was the fifth day of our expedition, and I was in the lead as we were pulling my sled over a stretch of flatter ice, maybe the only semi-flat section that day, when I decided it was time to stop and head back for Ryan's sled. I don't know why I chose that exact moment to halt. It wasn't like some warning signal lit up, saying "Danger, Eric Larsen, Danger." It just seemed like it was time. Each break from pulling the sled was gratifying; a momentary moratorium on our exhausting labor. This stop was different, though, as I turned to see the one sight you hope not to see on your way to the North Pole: a full-grown mother polar bear and her cub ambling straight toward us, less than 10 yards away. The terror was immediate. One swipe from the 12-inch-wide paws of an adult polar bear can be the first step to a painful death. For a split second, I was frozen in my tracks as one thought jumped to the forefront of my mind. *So this is how it ends, I am going to get eaten by polar bears.*

The two bears had been following us, walking in our footsteps, after having picked up our trail about 1,000 feet back. They were sniffing the air, attempting to figure out what these strange, multicolored creatures were and if we were edible. I quickly alerted Ryan and reached into my pocket to retrieve a pencil flare—a small signal flare that shoots a small explosive round into the air. Each of us kept one on hand for just such an occasion. As I fumbled with the flare, readying to fire, Ryan began to wave his poles and shout at the bears to scare them. After 18 years in the Arctic, I knew this could either be a good idea or a very bad one—polar bears are inherently curious, and his ruckus might make us irresistible. The fates were smiling. The bears paused for a moment—we were probably the first humans they had ever encountered, and Ryan's actions must have seemed very un-seal-like.

After a few seconds, they started back toward us. My heart was pounding. I frantically threaded the flare into the launcher and fired right over their heads. That stopped them dead in their tracks, but only for a few seconds. The yearling cub weighed several hundred pounds and was about three feet tall standing on all four feet, with two coal black eyes staring at us from its blank face. His eyes were sweeping over us and his ears were lifted toward the sky. His head tilted a bit to one side and up as he sniffed the air, before he decided we were too interesting to pass up and started toward us again, while momma stood watching. If we could not stop him, it was only a matter of time till she overcame her trepidation and decided to follow. Ryan launched his flare, stopping the cub less than 15 feet from us. We could see the steam rising from the young bear's skin, his nose moving slightly, inhaling our scent.

> Yes, we were food, but unlike seals, we were perilous to them.

This was the moment when lady luck smiled down upon us. Our one firearm, a 12-gauge shotgun, was in my sled, the one we were pulling. Frantically, I grabbed it, and, with blood racing, fired the first round over the bears' heads. It was a bear scare round, basically a very loud shell that shoots a bright, nonlethal, exploding round. That worked. Both of them took off back the way they had come. We had answered their question: Yes, we were food, but unlike seals, we were perilous to them.

The whole encounter took no longer than three minutes. But when it was happening, time slowed, and minutes seemed like hours. As the adrenaline washed over us, so, too, did the reality of the situation. After five days of frustrations and self-doubt over our slow progress, for that one moment everything went right. Our combined experience—my previous two North Pole expeditions and Ryan's two Mount Everest summits— allowed us both to keep clear heads when staring down one of the largest carnivores on the planet. The fact that we were pulling my sled and not

Ryan's meant that we had access to the gun. Stopping exactly when we did, before the bears were on us, when one swipe of their massive paws would have meant death. If any one of those things had not happened, we would have become a statistic.

If the struggles of the past five days had not driven home the message, the encounter with bears did. There was no question in either of our minds that we were in one of the most dangerous places on the face of the earth.

● ● ●

The day we met the polar bears was March 20, 2014, and Ryan and I were attempting what many have since dubbed one of the hardest and most dangerous expeditions on the planet. I don't argue with them. On my two previous cross-ice trips to the North Pole, I was pushed close to my breaking point. It is one of the harshest environments on earth. Nothing is static—everything is constantly changing daily, hourly. However prepared you are, something will inevitably go wrong. We were going to walk, ski, and swim (yes, swim) to the North Pole, unsupported. No dogsleds, no snowmobiles. Just the two of us dragging everything we needed behind us in two 317-pound sleds. We planned on being on the ice no more than 55 days. There would be no supplies awaiting us. Nothing would be waiting for us, except maybe more polar bears. The only time we would see anyone else would be if a plane either picked us up at our ultimate goal or evacuated us if things went very badly. In either case, having a plane reach us was anything but a certainty.

The North Pole's siren call has attracted adventurers for centuries.

The North Pole's siren call has attracted adventurers for centuries, due to its inaccessibility and continually changing conditions. Only 48

Overleaf: Ryan Waters trudges through pressure ice, pulling one of the team's 320 pound sleds.

individuals have ever successfully done what we were attempting. To put that in perspective, over 6,000 people have stood on top of Mount Everest. And with the rapid shrink of the ice pack starting to grab global attention and the ice itself at record levels of thinness, the terrain is becoming more unstable and dangerous.

The key to any successful expedition is having the right team, or in my case, the right teammate. I could not have asked for a better partner than Ryan. Levelheaded, good-tempered, and one of the preeminent mountain guides on the planet, he also conveniently lives in my hometown of Boulder, Colorado. He is the cofounder of Mountain Professionals, a guide company that leads people to the summits of the highest mountains in the world and to the poles. He has stood on top of all of the Seven Summits (the highest mountain on each continent), and completed the first ski traverse of Antarctica via the South Pole without resupply or the use of kites (often people use large kites to help pull them over the ice, it's a significant advantage). A successful North Pole trip would allow him to become the 10th person to complete the Explorers Grand Slam—the Seven Summits and both poles. Between the two of us, we had over 40 years of experience, and we hoped it would be enough.

Our specific goal was to ski from the tip of the northern Canadian coast, from Ellesmere Island, to the geographic North Pole, the 90th parallel. The spot where all of the longitude lines encircling the globe converge on maps. We were headed for the top of the planet. We would step onto the polar ice at Ellesmere Island, one of the northernmost pieces of land on the planet. From there we hoped to cover the 419 miles to the finish line in 48 days (requiring us to average 10 miles of skiing a day), thereby breaking the current "unsupported" speed record of 49 days, set by a Norwegian team in 2006.

> Our specific goal was to ski from the tip of the northern Canadian coast, from Ellesmere Island, to the geographic North Pole.

It was a gargantuan task, one that would require stamina, mental fortitude, and a healthy dose of luck. We would be facing temperatures that most people only have bad dreams about (30 to 40 below, with even lower windchill), Arctic storms that build in strength and can descend within hours, the continual drift of the ice pack to the south, polar bears, and, most importantly, ice that in recent decades has been getting thinner as climate change drastically affects the polar ice cap. All of these issues contributed to the fact that no one had successfully completed an over-ice expedition to the North Pole since 2010. Just the year before in 2013, not one team was able to even get onto the ice to attempt it. Continual bad weather patterns coupled with a smaller window of opportunity due to the summer melt beginning earlier each year had thwarted all of them from even getting a chance.

As temperatures slowly rise across the planet, one of the places they have the most impact is in the Arctic Ocean.

As temperatures slowly rise across the planet, one of the places they have the most impact is in the Arctic Ocean. The shrinking Arctic ice pack has been well documented in recent years and shows no signs of slowing. A report by researchers at the University of Washington found that the thickness of the ice pack has dropped a whopping 65 percent from 1975 to 2012, from 11.77 feet, on average, to 4.1 feet. On top of that, NASA recently announced that during the summer of 2012, the overall northern ice pack reached its smallest area of coverage ever: 1,389,967 square miles, compared with 3,088,817 in 1950 and 2,509,664 in 2000.[2] Many of my fellow polar explorers had been reiterating what the scientists were saying. The ice was getting thinner, and much, much more dangerous. This ice is unpredictable and can split apart more frequently, be prone to erratic drifts, and offer greater opportunities to fall through than the thicker multiyear pack ice of the past.

Overleaf: Ryan swimming across an opening in the melting Arctic sea ice.

As mentioned earlier, there is no land north of the 84th parallel. The geographic North Pole is just a coordinate on a map, unlike the South Pole, where there is a base and an actual pole that you can pose with for pictures. Without a GPS unit (or, historically, a sextant), you would never know if you were at the North Pole. Because the ice you are standing on moves constantly in the warmer months, any object placed in the ice at the North Pole would quickly be in the wrong location. Wind, tides, and currents all conspire to keep the ice sheets migrating. In our case, starting from Canada, they would be heading south, moving us in the wrong direction as we plodded north. We could wake up in our tent and find that while we were resting, the ice pack had transported us several miles farther away from our goal. It can be maddening.

Wind, tides, and currents all conspire to keep the ice sheets migrating.

The thinning ice pack is a big problem for expeditions. Leaner sheets of ice tend to break apart more easily, exposing the ocean hiding just underfoot. The openings, called leads, can be as narrow as a few feet or as wide as several football fields. There are only three choices when faced with maneuvering these. The first is to go around the lead. This can add hours to what would've taken minutes. Secondly, we could pitch our tent and hope the open water would freeze enough overnight to ski across. Lastly, we could don drysuits and swim to the other side through 29 degree seawater while towing our sleds behind us. Obviously this is the least preferred and most dangerous of our options, but would be unavoidable for our journey.

In addition to creating more leads, the other major challenge of thinning ice pack is the formation of more pressure ridges. The thicker the ice, the more stable it is. When ice sheets thin, they tend to break apart more—the tensile strength of the ice is not strong enough to hold them together. As the sheets pull apart and then crash back together, they

Right: the author, Eric Larsen, north of the 84th parallel

buckle and pile up blocks of ice into taller and taller heaps of rubble—kind of like how the collision of tectonic plates causes the formation of mountains, except that these changes can happen in the space of days. There have always been pressure ridges in the Arctic, but with the rapidly deteriorating ice shelf, we are seeing an exponential increase in these formations. And more pressure ridges means much slower and much harder travel.

Both Ryan and I knew before heading out that due to the rapidly deteriorating conditions, this expedition would be significantly harder than any we had ever attempted. In 2006, I was part of the team that first successfully reached the North Pole in summer, and I reached it again in 2010 when I became the first person to ever reach the South Pole, the North Pole, and the summit of Mount Everest in one year. I knew this expedition would probably be the last chance I would ever have to undertake this adventure. It is just becoming too dangerous. In fact, there was an excellent chance we would fail, as so many others have lately. In 2013, British ultrarunner Tim Williamson was planning to walk to and from the North Pole unsupported. It was a task I thought would be impossible. Turns out, it was: record warm temperatures scrubbed his attempt before it even started. The year before, in 2012, the Irish duo of Clare O'Leary and Mike O'Shea were forced to turn back after only a few weeks on the ice, due to a rough start and financial issues. So many things can come together to make the success rate for this trip plummet. I hoped and prayed that the fates would align for the two of us to make it, unlike so many others. I had experience dealing with the melting ice pack, and Ryan's résumé was impressive, but one never knows what will happen north of the Arctic Circle. One thing was certain: like it or not, the days of over-ice North Pole expeditions are coming to an end.

> I hoped and prayed that the fates would align for the two of us to make it, unlike so many others.

Chapter 1

Finally

Coordinates: 83 degrees north, 419 miles to North Pole

The first thing you notice in the Arctic is the cold; it's pervasive and brutal, and different from every other cold on the planet. Yet it is also one of the most important ingredients to a successful polar expedition. Cold defines everything here. Without the cold there is no ice, and without ice there are no more North Pole expeditions. There is no land here. The only way to reach the pole is to ski or snowshoe over sheets of floating ice. The climate in the polar regions creates a stark environment, and every visit reminds me what a special place this is and how lucky I am to experience it. This time was no different.

As I stepped down from the door of the De Havilland Twin Otter plane that had ferried me and my teammate Ryan Waters to this isolated stretch of coastline called Cape Discovery in the far northern regions of Canada, the blast of minus 31 degrees air was shocking. Yet the scenery was stunning. Standing on Ellesmere Island,[1] I saw directly ahead of me a smooth sheet of white gradually dropped down toward the Arctic Ocean. Where the land ended and the Arctic Ocean began was only discernible by the distant ridges of ice rubble piled up where the massive ocean sheets had been slowly smashed into the shore. Overhead the sky was a crystalline blue with a few clouds spread along the horizon. The sun was burning brightly, deceptively beckoning you to bask in it, but the frigid air overwhelmed what little warmth it offered. There is no warmth here. Behind us the mountains rose over a thousand feet from the ice and snow of the Discovery Ice Rise, a shelf of land ice fastened to the shore, on which we were standing. A wave of relief flooded over me. We were finally here.

Overleaf: The first of many Arctic selfies

After a multitude of delays and roadblocks, the adventure was about to begin. But in the pit of my stomach, there was another feeling—one of dread. I knew all too well what massive hardships and struggles lay in store for the next two months. We were attempting to do something that fewer than 50 people had ever successfully done. We were embarking on an unsupported journey[2] to the North Pole, dragging two sleds loaded down with every single bit of gear and food we would need. If everything worked out perfectly, we would reach the pole in less than 48 days and 22 hours, breaking the speed record set in 2006 by the Norwegian team of Cecilie Skog, Rolf Bae, and Per Henry Borch. Unfortunately, things rarely go perfectly in the Arctic.

There is no warmth here.

We weren't the only team disembarking from the plane, though. We had shared the flight, and its cost, with a team of two Norwegians—Lars Flesland and Kristoffer Glestad—who also, like us, were attempting to break the unsupported speed record to the North Pole. The two men were in their early twenties and incredibly fit, and were mounting this expedition between college classes back home. Impressive.

During our time prepping and packing gear in Resolute Bay[3] and awaiting our flight north, we got to know them, along with the members of the two other expeditions—Mike O'Shea and Clare O'Leary of Ireland, attempting a supported expedition, and Yasu Ogita of Japan, attempting an unsupported solo expedition—that were staging there. The fraternity of explorers is a small and, generally, a friendly one. There are not many who feel the call of the Arctic as acutely as we do. Still, the camaraderie is kept at an arm's distance. Sure, we swap stories and information while stuck in base areas, ogle each others' gear. But polar adventurers are, by their nature, solitary and independent. No one is looking for last-minute "tips" on gear or travel strategies. While I may have been on the ice the most, no one was asking for advice, and I wasn't giving it. It's a weird dynamic, so it's best to just block others out of your mind and focus on your own tasks.

The fraternity of explorers is a small and, generally, a friendly one.

Naming the sled

Another blast of frigid air abruptly took me out of my moment of introspection and brought me back to the present. The pilot, Terry, a bull of a man with a full beard, wanted to get the plane unloaded as quickly as possible so he and his copilot could be off the ice and begin their five-hour return flight back to Resolute Bay. I fumbled with my neoprene face mask, trying to secure the velcro behind my head. My fingers quickly became numb with cold from the effort. I swung my arms in wide pinwheels, hoping to drive warm blood to my fingertips. As the feeling began to return, I moved to set up our Sony camcorder to film the scene as we unloaded. In a few more seconds, my fingers were painfully cold, and I paused to frantically spin my arms again before hitting record.

Lifting our Arctic Challenge 230 Kevlar Pulk sleds out of the plane is an effort. They measure 7.5 feet long and weigh 16.5 pounds empty, but we transported them half-filled, making them over 200 pounds each. They were loaned to us and had already seen service on another North Pole expedition. We had gotten to know these sleds intimately over the past few months as we customized them—adding new runners, repairing chips with graphite epoxy, and installing new custom covers. Our sleds were our base camp; they would carry everything we needed to survive on the ice for nearly two months. We had even named them. Mine was christened the *HMS Merritt,* after my 18-month-old son back home in Colorado. It seemed fitting to scrawl his name on the back of my sled. I have hopes of imbuing my love of the outdoors in him. Ryan's sled still bore the name *Polar Princess,* bestowed by its previous owner Cecilie Skog; it was a source of good-natured ribbing between us.

The correct sled setup can be the tipping point (in a long line of tipping points) between success or failure on the ice. Instead of opting for the more traditional setup of two smaller sleds each, we had decided to use Arctic Challenge 230s. With smaller sleds, you split your gear and ferry one forward, leave it, and head back for the other. It is kind of an extreme version of leapfrog. The benefit of that system is that we each

Out on the ice, isolated from every living soul and store on the planet, we would have to fend for ourselves.

would have pulled our own sleds—not teaming up to drag one big sled together. The fact that not buying four small sleds saved us $16,000 was a big part of our decision, but I also did not want to end up abandoning two of them halfway through the trip, once they were no longer needed—a common tactic of polar expeditions, where excess weight is unwanted weight. Instead we would each pull 320 pounds of gear behind us in the beginning, a choice I hoped we would not regret. As Ryan and I started to repack our sleds with the rest of our gear, I questioned my frugality and ethics in going with one sled each. They were going to be damn heavy.

People take common things for granted. Light, heat, and chairs all seem so simple in our modern society. Out on the ice, isolated from every living soul and store on the planet, we would have to fend for ourselves. If something broke, we would have to fix it. If we got injured, we would have to deal with it. If we needed water, we would have to melt ice to make it. In planning this expedition, both Ryan and I had painstakingly gone over every item we needed, weighing its pros and cons. Every calorie was accounted for; each piece of gear had an express purpose. If we could trim a few ounces of weight and still maintain the integrity of an item, we did. Knowing we would be dragging everything behind us for almost two months provided all the motivation we needed to pare down our gear. As we started to load our sleds, I was amazed at how much we were able to fit in them.

Basic Team Gear

2 sets Asnes Amundsen skis plus one extra backup ski

Rottefella 3-pin expedition bindings (one extra pair in repair kit)

2 sets MSR Lightning Ascent 25-inch snowshoes with custom MSR bindings to work in the cold

2 sets MSR Flight trekking poles, customized

2 Arctic Challenge 230 Kevlar Pulk sleds with custom Granite Gear sled cover

2 Granite Gear Pulk harnesses, customized

1 set of Polar Picks

2 Helly Hansen drysuits

1 Hilleberg Keron 3 GT tent

2 MSR Responder shovels

2 MSR XGK EX stoves

MSR WhisperLite International stove (backup)

MSR fuel pumps, customized

MSR Dual-handle 5.3L hard-anodized aluminum pot

MSR Heat Exchanger, customized

Stove board, customized

8 MSR 30 oz. fuel bottles with expedition fuel cap

13.2 gallons White Gas (14 cans per sled)

2 tent brushes

2 Sleeping-bag systems—Nemo Equipment Canon -40 (down), Mezzo Loft 30 (synthetic)

Overleaf: The author in Resolute Bay, wearing his drysuit

Sony NEX-VG30H camcorder

24 Pencil flares and 2 launchers

Mossberg 500 pump action pistol grip shotgun

Shells for shotgun

Repair kit

First-aid kit

3 ice screws

4 snow stakes

100-foot rope

2 AA battery chargers with DC plugs, custom designed to charge phones and camera batteries.

300 AA batteries (to power cameras)

2 Suunto MC-2 World Balanced compasses

DeLorme inReach 2 way communicator

Garmin eTrex Vista HCX 1 GPS

2 iPhones

2 PalmPilots (1 backup)

Iridium 9505a Satellite phone

Iridium 9555 Satellite phone (backup)

2 Sony NEX-6 cameras

2 Sony Action Cams

1 Nokia Lumia 1020 Windows phone

2 Tripods

Granite Gear 1-quart insulated cell block

Stanley 1-quart mug/bowl

Stanley 1-quart insulated flask

2 Stanley insulated food jars

Personal Gear

Integral Designs Vapor Barrier bag liner

RidgeRest Solar sleeping pad

Sierra Designs Bivy bag

Alfa Extreme 75mm boots

Outdoor Research Brooks Ranger overboots—customized

3 ExOfficio Men's Give-N-Go Sport Mesh 6″ boxer briefs
Helly Hansen Dry ¾ pants
2 Helly Hansen Dry pants
2 Helly Hansen Warm pants
Helly Hansen Pace Short Sleeve
2 Helly Hansen Warm Ice crew shirts
Helly Hansen Dry shirt
2 Helly Hansen Warm Ice half-zips
Helly Hansen H2 Flow jacket
Bergans Arctic Expedition jacket
Bergans Arctic Expedition bibs
Bergans Expedition Down Light jacket
Mountain Hardwear Compressor insulated pants
Sierra Designs DriZone Down Booties
2 sets of Wigwam Merino AirLite Pro socks
2 sets of Wigwam Glove liners
Bergans Finse mitten shells
2 sets Apocalypse Designs fleece mittens
Brenig polar over-mittens
2 MSR knit hats
Outdoor Research windproof balaclava
Ergodyne 813 fleece utility gloves
Ergodyne 819WP Thermal Waterproof Gauntlet, custom
Ergodyne Multi-Band buff
Zeal Optics Slate Goggles, custom nose beak

Personal Food

125 Mountain House Freeze dinner meals
3.85 pounds butter
100 Pro Bars
50 Builder Bars
50 Clif Bars
50 Clif Mojo Bars
50 Clif Shot Bloks

1.65 pounds dried soup mix

11 pounds of Rittersport chocolate

5.5 pounds salami

5.5 pounds of cheddar cheese

2.2 pounds macadamia mixed nuts

150 pieces Skratch Labs candy

300 servings Skratch Labs drink mix

1.18 gallons olive oil

4 cans Pringles

3 bags cheese puffs we bought in Resolute Bay (for celebrations)

25 servings freeze-dried ice cream

5 days' worth of emergency rations

In 15 minutes, everything was unloaded from the plane and we exchanged goodbyes with the pilot and copilot. They climbed back in the cockpit, fired the engines, and immediately turned to taxi toward the spot where the plane's skis first touched down. The prop wash stabbed icy needles through our clothes, and we leaned away from the blast, worried about both frostbite and our gear blowing away. The plane spun again; facing toward us, and after a surprisingly short amount of time, throttled up and began bouncing toward us. I still had the camera rolling when the plane lifted off, and then tipped a wing in our direction to say goodbye. It was so close we both ducked.

> It's a scary moment knowing that your lifeline is completely severed.

I watched the plane circle around to the south and fly back toward Eureka, the whine of engines fading to nothing in the distance. It's a scary moment knowing that your lifeline is completely severed, if you need evacuation you might have to wait days for a plane to arrive. But there wasn't much time for self-reflection now. The cold was seeping in fast and we needed to get moving.

Less than five minutes later, the Norwegian team walked over to us, wished us good luck, and skied off for the North Pole. Quickly they were just blips on the horizon. They had opted to go with much smaller sleds than ours and were pulling only 240 pounds behind them, instead of the 317 pounds we were each dragging. They seemed like finely tuned race cars compared with our used minivan style. My first thought was, "We're screwed, those kids are going to fly to the pole and crush the record." They had consulted all the right people beforehand, their gear was impressive, and they were in prime shape. But just as quickly, I drove that thought out of my mind. This was my third time heading out on the ice of the North Pole—I had successfully completed the first ever summertime expedition in 2006, and again reached the pole in 2010. And if those expeditions taught me anything, it was to block out all distractions and focus solely on the task at hand. The ice of the North Pole is one of the most dangerous places on the earth; losing focus can be deadly.

The first moments were tough, getting our sleds to move.

We recorded a final video, but both Ryan and I were at a loss to find any deep meaning. "It's time to stop talking and start skiing," I proclaimed, and turned the camera off. Ryan tucked it into his sled. The sleds were so full; it was difficult to zip the covers closed. Once again I was filled with regret; we should have brought our smaller second sled system to split up the weight. Oh well, nothing we can do now.

We clipped our harnesses into the tug line—a long, adjustable line on the back of our harness—and leaned into the weight. Since the slope was smooth heading downhill to the ocean ice, we headed out on our skis. I knew from previous experience that once we hit the jumbled ice wreckage at the edge of the sea ice, we would have to switch to snowshoes for traction and maneuverability. But at the moment it was a pleasure to be sliding along on our skis. The first moments were tough, getting our sleds to move. They felt anchored. Our skis slid in place, useless against the weight until we could apply enough torque to break the sleds free. Then they popped loose and off we went.

The view was amazing heading down the ice rise. As far as my eyes could see was the flattish surface of the ocean ice disappearing over the horizon. Ryan and I looked at one another. I knew that under his face mask there was a smile, just like mine.

"It's cold, let's head out toward the ice," I heard him say. I agreed. We had 50 days to make it to the pole; every minute standing around is wasted. Time to head north. The adventure begins. My fear about our sleds disappeared; they will be fine. We could see the Norwegians' tracks veer slightly off to the west. For one beautiful mile everything was perfect. All of our planning, all of our training, all of our preparations, everything we had been doing for the past 24 months had coalesced into this one singular moment.

> When ocean ice floes hit land, it causes a violent upheaval of ice.

The closer we got to the edge of the ice, a large rubble field took shape. Unlike my expedition in 2010, when large gaps of open water between the sea ice and the land-fast ice of the shore caused us fits figuring out how to get out onto the ice, the ice sheets this year are right next to shore but look rough. When I saw this on the flight in, it gave me hope. I knew we could get off land quickly and onto the ice cap. Traversing the broken ice near shore would be tough, but at least we would be heading in the right direction. What I could not see from high in the air was the overall chaos and destruction that awaited us. When ocean ice floes hit land, it causes a violent upheaval of ice. The leading edges shatter and are shoved into the air at random angles. When the next floe behind it continues to exert pressure, more of the ice fractures, piling higher and higher. This can continue for miles out from the shore, deep into the ice field. As the pressure causes successive floes of ice to break apart and slam together, it forms incessant pressure ridges. These angular ice blocks pile high above and below the ocean, creating barriers that can tower as high as 20 feet. Navigating your way through them can be frustrating, exhausting, and dangerous.

At the bottom of the ice rise, we were forced to halt. Continuing forward on our skis would be impossible; we would need snowshoes. The rubble was all-encompassing. Just finding an entrance in was daunting.

No longer were we able to see the horizon—we were at the same level as the ice. After a few minutes of walking horizontally along the barrier, I climbed to the top of a ridge. I could see a way in that would fit our sleds. Ryan and I scarfed down energy bars and headed through a tight rift between two looming blocks of ice. Within the first 40 feet my sled became stuck. I had to lean

I was stuck. We had only traveled 60 feet.

as far forward as possible, straining against my harness. My legs were quivering, but the sled would not advance over a block of ice. Gritting my teeth, I threw all of my weight forward and it sprang free. There was no time for celebration, I had momentum and must keep moving. Twenty feet ahead of me, the pathway climbed five feet over a pile of fractured ice blocks; it looked like a pile of white Legos discarded by a giant child. I started climbing up, pulling my sled behind me. I made it about three feet up before my sled ground to a halt. Try as I might, it would not budge. I was stuck. We had only traveled 60 feet.

I turned to look back and Ryan was behind me, panting from the effort he had put in to get here. If he was struggling as much as I was, I knew we were going to have to adapt our methods. I am five-eight and 155 pounds—not a big man, but when you are traversing ice, bigger often is not better. After over a decade and a half partaking in expeditions across the globe, I am in decent shape. Ryan was the strong man on our expedition. His six-two frame and 190 pounds gave him an obvious advantage early in the trip, pulling a fully laden sled. He had been guiding on big mountains for close to two decades. With his longer brown hair and beard, he looked the part of an adventurer, while I had buzzed my hair short and shaved right before we left Resolute Bay. Though I looked like the middle-aged father that I was, looks can be deceiving. I was the one with the knowledge on this trip. I had been here before.

"We are going to have to double-pull the sleds, unfortunately," I told Ryan. It was something we knew was a distinct possibility heading into the trip. Ryan reluctantly agreed. This was not a decision entered into lightly; in fact we dreaded it.

The premise of double-pulling the sleds is simple; both of us hook our harnesses into one sled and pull it forward—like a team of sled dogs. I would be slightly ahead of Ryan, so we would have space to maneuver. Our combined strength would propel the sleds up and over obstacles. It sounds easier than it is. You are forever banging into each other, falling over as the ice shifts and crumbles underfoot, while vigilantly monitoring the 317-pound sled, trying to keep it from sliding into the back of your legs, causing a potentially expedition-ending injury. It is horrible. When things got too steep or particularly crappy, one of us would unhook and have to push or lift the sled from behind. Smashed fingers and fractures are common on trips like ours, from muscling sleds up and over pressure ridges, ice blocks, and drifts.

Working together we are able to move my sled forward 600 feet over the next half-hour. Often I would unhook and scout ahead to find a pathway that did not dead-end. The key was to continually head north. Thank God for my compass; out in that fractured landscape, you can easily get turned around. Parking the sled in a small clearing, we turned to walk back south to get the other one. One of the scarier things you can do in the Arctic is leave your sled—even just to walk 600 feet. It is your lifeboat in a frozen sea. Lose it and you die, it's that simple.

> Smashed fingers and fractures are common on trips like ours.

The only positive about double-pulling sleds is that you get a breather every time you walk back to the one you left. But for every step we traverse north, we are actually traveling triple the distance—forward with the first sled, back to get the second sled, and forward again. For us to move both sleds forward 600 feet, we traveled 1,800 feet. It is a literal example of taking a step forward and two steps back. Double-pulling, for us, was a necessary evil. It drastically slowed our forward progress and could realistically have sabotaged any chance we had of reaching the pole in 48 days. But for the moment, we had no choice. As we dragged the second sled forward, a sense of dread settled upon me. We were already over a week behind schedule attempting something most people would consider impossible. Now within minutes of hitting the ice we were double-pulling? How could we possibly succeed?

● ● ●

I have always been drawn to the outdoors. As a kid growing up in Wisconsin, I spent as much of my time as possible running around outside, often in subfreezing temperatures. My father was the director of a local nature center, so I was always getting involved in one adventure or another. After graduating from St. Olaf College in 1993, I was guiding whitewater trips and working as a bike mechanic when fate presented me with an opportunity that set me on a pathway to the ends of the world: I was hired to work as a dog musher for a wilderness lodge in northern Minnesota. Never mind that I had never driven a team of dogs in my life. I was a quick learner and soon discovered I loved it. If you had asked me then, I would have said that I'd be a dog musher for the rest of my life. Over the next several years, I spent summers guiding in Colorado and winters mushing dogs in Minnesota and beyond. When I was hired on for a monthlong trip in the upper Northwest Territories in 1995, I got my first glimpse into the Arctic. It was amazing, traveling across the vast expanse of the treeless Arctic in places that I had read about as a kid. At night the northern lights stretched from one horizon to the other in a rainbow of colors. I was hooked and wanted more.

Toward the end of the nineties, I had been working for four years as a full-time adventure and science coordinator for a nature center in northern Minnesota. That job made me realize I wanted to tell people the story of the wilderness, to share with others the love I have for being outdoors.

Overleaf: The author looks back at Ryan and the sleds as he tries to find a path through the ice.

Fast-forward a few more years and jobs, and I found myself working as base-camp manager and education director on a dogsled expedition going from Churchill, Manitoba, all the way to Ellesmere Island. It was my second big dogsled expedition north of the border. This time we were exploring the Hudson Bay region, which really is true Arctic conditions. But then the dot-com bubble popped, the company I was working with failed, and I found myself working in Grand Marais, Minnesota, a tiny town located on the North Shore of Lake Superior, just miles from Canada. That was where I met fellow resident Lonnie Dupre in 2002. Over beers we both started talking about doing something different, something undone in polar expeditions.

After nearly four years of planning and preparation, I completed my first North Pole expedition in 2006 with Lonnie. To this day, our One World Expedition is the first and only successful summer excursion to the North Pole. The idea was simple: draw the world's attention to the melting ice pack up north by having a boat in a place that most people think is permanently frozen. Lonnie, 10 years my senior, had racked up a long list of Arctic expeditions by the time we met and had just completed a multiyear "circumnavigation" of Greenland. Good-natured and jolly, I knew there was no way I could plan and raise funds for a trip this big on my own. Lonnie's expertise and experience would be integral to our trip. In reality, it was an apprenticeship for me. When it was done, I realized that expeditions were the perfect platform to advocate for the environment.

In 2008, I led my first expedition to the South Pole, becoming one of the few Americans to have skied to both poles. In November 2009, I embarked on my most ambitious endeavor: the Save the Poles Expedition. Over the following 12 months, I would become the first person to ever ski to both poles and summit Mount Everest (often called the third pole) in one year. When I reached the summit of Everest on October 15,

> To this day, our One World Expedition is the first and only successful summer excursion to the North Pole.

2010, elated and tired, I had successfully completed the triple crown of polar explorers and set another world record.

But there was one significant difference between all of the previous expeditions and the one I was on with Ryan: all of those trips were supported, with supplies waiting for me on the way, allowing me to move quicker and put less stress on my body. The expedition we were on now, with no outside support, would test me in completely new ways.

During the planning of my Save the Poles trip, I met Ryan through mutual friends in Boulder, Colorado. I had just moved there from Minnesota to train and, equally important, nurture a burgeoning relationship with my girlfriend at the time, Maria Hennessey. Having absolutely no high-altitude experience, I knew that climbing Denali in Alaska would provide the perfect training ground for me. Ryan offered to guide me to the summit. As the co-owner and founder of Mountain Professionals, he is one of the preeminent mountain guides on the planet. He has stood atop the highest points on each continent, known as the Seven Summits, plus numerous other peaks across the globe. While we climbed the mountain, he taught me what I needed to know for Everest and, at the same time, I helped pique his interest in Arctic exploration.

When I started the first leg of the Save the Poles trip in Antarctica, Ryan was there with his girlfriend at the time, Cecilie Skog, the Norwegian explorer who was part of the team that set the unsupported North Pole record in 2006. (It's funny how things link up in life sometimes.) While I was embarking on my race to the poles, they skied 1,117 miles across the continent via the South Pole in 70 days to set the record for the longest unsupported ski traverse of Antarctica. Ryan and I were good friends by then and had discussed him joining me on my North Pole leg of the trip that year. But after his traverse across the southernmost continent, he was just too worn out.

Once I completed Save the Poles, I spent several months doing the talking-head circuit, educating the public on the plight of the poles and discussing my trip. But, as always seems to happen, I started to grow restless. There were two big ideas that kept creeping into my consciousness. The first was to become the first person to ride a bike to the South

Pole. The second was, surprisingly, to go back to the Arctic Ocean and the North Pole.

Two years later, during late December 2012, I spent 17 days riding into and out of the interior of Antarctica alone on a custom fat bike during my failed Cycle South Expedition. Although I did not accomplish my goal of reaching the South Pole, I did make it close to 150 miles inland before being forced to turn back due to soft snow conditions. At the time, it was the longest bike expedition on the continent. Had I not already been simultaneously planning the North Pole expedition with Ryan, I would have tried again the next season. But I was singularly focused on the Arctic. It was something I desperately wanted to try. Both of my previous successful trips to the northernmost point on earth had required supply drops and, frankly, that irked me a bit. It was time to see if I could make it in a more elegant style, reminiscent of the classical expeditions before GPS, satellite phones, and airdrops—just a small team alone on the ice with no outside help. Equally important to me was my over decade-long quest to tell the story of climate change in the Arctic: the polar ice cap was melting at an alarming rate, and the world hardly even took notice. A quick call to Ryan confirmed that he was in for the trip, and we started the planning in earnest.

> But, as always seems to happen, I started to grow restless.

After much deliberation, we decided to call it the Last North Expedition. There was good reason to choose this moniker. With the shrinking ice cap and a shorter winter season, soon there will not be enough ice to successfully make the crossing. From 2005 to 2010, seven expeditions made the crossing unsupported, but no one had been able to pull it off since. Thin ice, large sections of open water, erratic weather patterns, and rough terrain had thwarted team after team. In fact, only one group of Russians made it to the pole, and that was in modified buses that could float. Leave it to the Russians to take a floating bus to the North Pole— you have to give them style points. Our expedition, however, would be quite a bit different, and we were quickly finding out exactly how difficult it would be.

As the polar ice packs melt, several things are happening concurrently to make expedition travel harder and more dangerous. Scientists recently released a study that shows that the annual mean thickness of the ice has gone from 11.78 feet in 1975 to 4.1 feet in 2012.[4] While four feet of ice seems pretty thick, and it is, it still represents a reduction of 65 percent during that time frame. Thin ice is much less stable, and the floes are prone to break apart. When this happens, it forms the leads[5] that present barriers that can continually pop up, blocking your way. You have three choices when confronted with them: you can wait for the water to refreeze, go around them, or swim across them. All are time-consuming. When the ice sheet was much thicker, it was inherently more stable and you could travel for days sometimes without confronting a lead. Now you are lucky to go a few hours without seeing one. Plus, when the ice was thicker, it was less responsive to the ocean currents ever present under your feet. The lighter an object, the more it moves around in the water. The thinning ice sheets have unmoored from most coastlines except those of Greenland and the Canadian Northwest Territories. So we are confronted with free-floating ice, usually headed toward North America—it can move several kilometers each day under your feet in the wrong direction—and floes that break apart and crash together, creating mini mountain ranges of ice. Toss in the fact that the Arctic summer melt is starting about three days earlier each year, and you can see that soon it will be impossible to travel across the cap the way explorers did in the past.

The initial plan was to launch the trip in late winter of 2013, just a few months after I returned from my South Pole bike trip, but then life got in the way. When I found out my wife Maria was pregnant in the summer of 2012, I knew she would need me at home, not off traipsing across the ice while she was changing diapers as a "single parent." So we delayed until early 2014. While my son Merritt learned to crawl and then walk, Ryan and I dove headlong into trip preparations.

There is a lot that goes into launching an expedition. You don't just head to the local travel agent and book one. While we spent the summer of 2013 accumulating gear and training in the mountains surrounding

Boulder, we also were beating the bushes looking for sponsors. We knew that we would need close to $200,000 to pull off the trip; half that was just to pay for our flight off the ice at journey's end. That's a lot of cash, which neither of us had. I often like to say this about polar travel: it's the most expensive way to have a bad time ever devised. Sponsors are what make these types of trips possible. They donate gear, help defray travel costs, and allow you to publicize the adventure as it unfolds. After spending over a decade planning trips like these, I am accustomed to the seat-of-your-pants lifestyle that envelops you in the months leading up to the go date. Funding inevitably comes in at the 11th hour. In 2010, after I returned from the South Pole on the first leg of the Save the Poles trip, all of my time was dedicated to raising the cash needed to fund the next leg. By the time we left for the Last North Expedition a few months later, I was mentally exhausted from the never-ending strain of soliciting sponsorships. The stress of fund-raising often eclipses all other worries.

Luckily, in October, Animal Planet reached out and asked us if we would be willing to produce a TV show about our journey. I had been planning on filming the entire trip to help publicize the plight of the region, and Animal Planet was the perfect medium to maximize the impact. Once we nailed down its

> The stress of fund-raising often eclipses all other worries.

participation, the fund-raising became slightly easier. The exposure that it offered enabled us to close the deal with several other groups, including a small partnership with both Microsoft and Sony.

In between sending innumerable e-mails searching for money, we started accumulating the impressive list of gear we would need. Many hours were spent debating the merits of one set of skis versus another, what baselayer to bring, and how much food would be needed. Since the two of us had each spent more than a decade scaling mountains and traipsing across polar landscapes, some of the decisions were easy (I knew my MSR XKG stove was coming; it's amazing) and some were hard (my trusty Granite Gear harness was showing some wear and tear). Many of the items we modified to strip off excess ounces—rimming metal zipper pulls, removing the netting from our tent—but others we were adding to, like giving our trekking poles a second set of grips halfway down the shaft for climbing over pressure ridges. My house, much to Maria's chagrin, became the staging area, many rooms spread with items, several in various stages of repair or modification.

Then there was the training. From previous experience, I knew that the race to the pole is not a sprint but a long, drawn-out sufferfest. Therefore I focused on strength-endurance sessions and mimicking the types of things we'd be doing on the ice. Spending long hours on the bike (both mountain and road) as well as hiking with a weighted pack in Colorado's mountainous terrain helped create a solid base. Our favorite training method, however, was simple and straightforward: pulling tires. Attaching two large truck tires to our harness, we would struggle up hillsides mimicking the stress we would be dealing with on the ice while towing our sleds. Before packing up, we would also engage in a series of CrossFit-type drills—throwing and flipping our tires and running with them to hone our core, upper body, and what we jokingly referred to as old man strength. It was hellish and hard but paid dividends later on. But there was one nagging issue in the back of my mind that I worried might haunt us during the expedition. We were not getting enough Arctic training for the daunting epic we were about to attempt. Between me being a new father and Ryan running trips for Mountain Professionals, we were not able to set aside enough time to train the way I thought we should, on actual ice. My biggest fear was that Ryan had never been on polar ice before. Sure, he had summited some of the largest mountains in the world and traversed Antarctica three years earlier, but that was all on land. Ice sheets are an entirely different—and much more dangerous—environment. And I knew from past trips that trekking to the North Pole was 10 times worse than the South Pole.

We were able to set aside two weeks that spring to train in Svalbard, Norway, in polar conditions. We tested out the skis, snowshoes, sleds, and other gear we were thinking of bringing on the expedition. Overall it was a successful outing, except for one issue: we did not spend any time on actual polar floes. All of our time was spent on land-based ice and snow. It was something that I would regret later on.

But all of the time spent pulling tires up mountainsides in the summer heat, the heartburn from fund-raising, and the endless modifications on our gear were all worth it. I knew I would be able to bring back the story of the Arctic ice cap to people before it is gone. That's a price I will willingly pay over and over.

The last two months before we left Boulder were a blur. If I slept more than five hours a night, I was lucky. The hardest part was saying goodbye to my family. It always gets tense between Maria and I before I leave. Part is driven by her worries for my safety, part is overflow from the chaos of organizing the expedition, and part is due to the financial strains it can put on us. We have been together since 2008, so she is no rookie to this expedition thing. During the Save the Poles project, I was gone for half a year in total. But this time was different. I was the father of an 18-month-old, and I was leaving my family to head to one of the more dangerous places on the planet, somewhere I had already been twice. Maria was going to be on her own for over two months with a precocious little boy while I was off adventuring. Many times she questioned the intelligence of this endeavor. Even our last night together was stressful. After putting Merritt to bed, we repacked freeze-dried meals in our living room. I didn't even get to sleep. I was up all night packing the remaining gear items. Just before the shuttle arrived to pick me up early the next morning, I snuck quietly into Merritt's room for one final look. Then I gave Maria a hug that I knew might be my last. Leaving the two of them was one of the hardest things I have ever done.

It took us three flights spread over two days—Denver to Ottawa, Ottawa to Iqaluit, Iqaluit to Resolute Bay—to put us within a thousand miles of the starting line. On the flight into Resolute Bay, Ryan told me about a feeling of nagging dread he was experiencing.

"If we were heading to a mountain right now I would feel 100 percent confident," he said. "But despite all of my other expeditions, the North Pole is an unknown to me." I understood his feelings, but for the first time in months, I was feeling relaxed. We had begun.

Right: Ryan sealing the seams of the team's drysuits

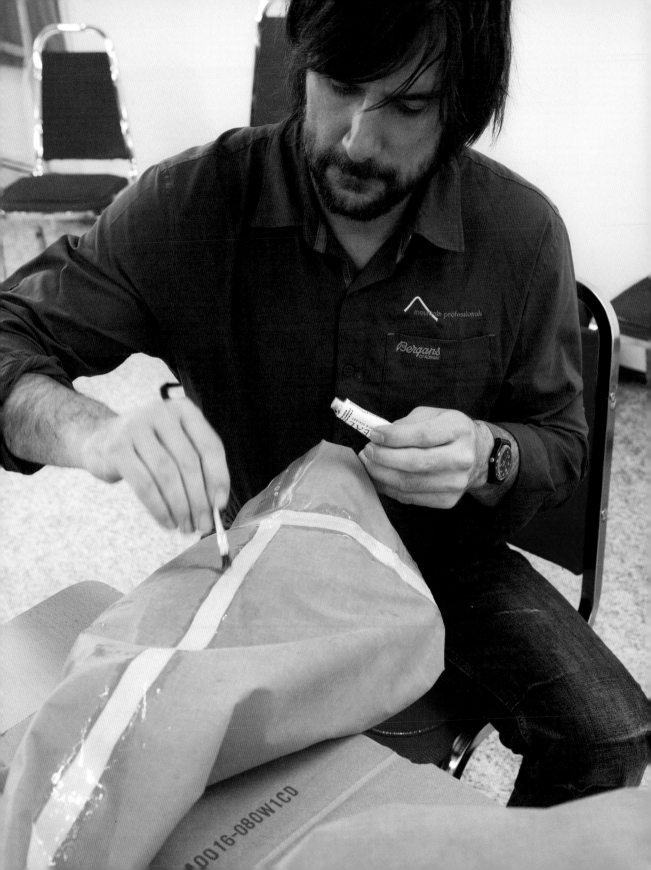

The author (left) and Ryan killing time in Resolute Bay

Upon arrival in Resolute Bay, on March 2, the two of us become a whirlwind of activity. Luckily all of our gear arrived with us, which is not a given in expedition travel. There were only five days to finish preparations and last-minute modifications to our gear before our planned departure date, March 7.

There is not much to do in Resolute Bay, a small Inuit village of 242 people on the Northwest Passage. It's not the end of the world, but you sure can see it from there. It's just a small frontier town in this white noth-ingness on the Arctic Ocean, and it has a year-round average temperature of three degrees. From our staging area in the South Camp Inn, the two of us spend 12 hours a day preparing. One of the main tasks is to indi-vidually portion and repack all of our food to remove excess packaging and add extra calories (butter and olive oil). We need to ensure that we have enough calories in the right proportion of proteins, carbohydrates, and fats to provide us enough energy for our journey. As the trip goes on, our daily caloric needs will increase dramatically, eventually reaching nearly 8,000 calories per person. So we pack food in three separate categories: 5 days of "starter" meals, 25 days of meals of with 6,500 calories, and 20 days with meals in the 7,500 to 8,000 range. Food prep is equally important—I know of at least one expedition that ended because someone cut his or her hand while trying to slice frozen cheese. So we cut one hundred portions of salami and cheese, which we will eat for lunch each day. Like so many other items, even our 11 pounds of chocolate—over 27,000 calories—must be prepared.

The reports we are getting about the ice are mixed. Some say it's not too bad, others say it's pretty broken up. When Ryan gets a little worried about the lack of concrete information, I remind him that there is so much that can happen between now and the start, everything could change. Plus, realistically, it's all bad ice. Accepting that the conditions will never improve is the first step to successfully reaching the pole.

Each night I message with Maria and Merritt while I still can. Overall, our mood is good leading up to departure. But then, as it always seems to on trips like these, things go sideways.

On March 6, the Japanese and Irish teams did not fly out as planned. Weather issues had forced a delay in their flight. Since they were ahead of us in the queue for a flight that meant we would also be delayed. Kenn Borek Air had the teams on a holding pattern waiting until it was safe to fly them up to Cape Discovery. They would be attempting to head north the next day, March 7, the day we were supposed to leave. Since 1970, Kenn Borek Air had been ferrying people around the Canadian Arctic, and this is the only flight service that could get us to where we needed to go. They are most definitely the experts, and when one of their pilots tells you it's not safe to fly, you listen. So on March 7, the flight departed in beautiful weather while we and the Norwegian team sat in the South Camp Inn, nervously checking and rechecking our gear, hoping that the window would hold so we could take off the next day.

When we went to check in the next morning, we were told two of the worst things I could imagine. The first was that the Canadian Ice Service

Overleaf: Resolute Bay at night. It's as cold as it looks.

had issued a weather warning, saying that Ellesmere Island was socked in by a storm. We would not be flying out and would have to wait another day. Due to the fact that the planes land on an ice shelf, with the absence of a marked runway, in the middle of nowhere, conditions have to be perfect for pilots to attempt such a dangerous flight. They literally attempt a couple of light landings and takeoffs using their landing skis to test the ice before they actually land. One mishap due to poor lighting or rough surface conditions and the plane could flip. Equally as distressing was the news that we were going to be overweight once our gear and the Norwegians' was loaded. This sent my already precarious mood plummeting. The pressure of trimming our gear at the 11th hour was too much. I wanted to give up and go home. Ryan was calm and levelheaded while he listened to me rant. Once I had it out of my system, we sat down and came up with a solution. Both teams would fly together for the first leg of the flight to Eureka, a weather station on Ellesmere Island where the plane would have to land to refuel. Once there, the plane would shuttle each team over at a time, thus eliminating the problem of the plane being too heavy to land on the snow.

A quick note about the cost of the flight to Cape Discovery: Every team is required to pay in advance for delivery to the start line and pickup at the finish. It costs $45,000 to fly to Ellesmere Island, but we were able to split that with the Norwegians. To get picked up at the pole, however, was an additional $110,000. So before we even left, we had to fork over $130,000. While the pickup fee is prorated if you have to be retrieved earlier, that does not offer much consolation. It's still a substantial amount. The financial pressure is with you every day on the ice.

Over the course of the week, we keep getting the same news. Inclement weather somewhere along the flight path has forced yet another delay. Call back tomorrow. Hopefully we would fly out then. Delays are an inevitable fact of these types of expeditions. Mother Nature is seldom cooperative. On the positive side, we were able to get some much-needed sleep—and, much to Maria's relief, I finished my taxes. Still, it was hard to be cooped up with all our gear packed as each day we were delayed ate into our potential window for successfully reaching the pole.

In the hotel, prepping 50 portions of salami and cheese for daily fuel on the ice

Equally worse, each day in Resolute Bay meant that we were spending over $200 a day per person to stay at the South Camp Inn.

In the past, there were three ways to get off the ice after reaching the pole. The first was simple: turn around and ski back. But that has only happened twice in history. The shrinking ice pack has forever closed the door on that option. The ice is just too dangerous. The second was to be picked up by helicopter at the pole and then head to Borneo, the Russian temporary base located roughly 80 miles away from the pole. From there you can catch a flight to Longyearbyen, Norway. In the past, the ice "island" that Borneo was on could support logistic operations until May, but a warming climate and deteriorating ice conditions meant that Borneo was closing earlier and earlier. In 2010, Borneo's end date was April 25. This year it would be gone by April 21. If we had left on our planned date of March 7, to get to Borneo we would have had only 46 days to reach the North Pole—a nearly impossible figure. So that left door number three, the only realistic option: getting picked up by airplane at the

The world famous Eureka International Airport. It was minus 40 when Eric and Ryan arrived.

Pole, or somewhere close. Of course, there was one unfortunate caveat: the latest date that Kenn Borek Air would commit to picking anyone up was May 4. That gave us 59 days to complete the crossing. Our goal was 48 days, but we were realistic enough about our chances to assume it would take longer. We were only going to take enough full rations for 50 days, with five days of emergency food. It was a huge gamble, but one we were willing to take. Regardless, we had set a target of 48 to 52 days to reach the pole, but every day that ticked by in Resolute Bay ate into the cushion of time we needed to safely reach the pole. If we did not get out by March 15, we would have to store our gear, head back home, and hopefully come back the next year—something that could never be guaranteed to happen.

On the night of March 14, we finally received a good forecast. It was looking like we might actually be flying out the next morning. We borrowed an old beat-up truck and drove all of our gear and the Norwegians'

Fuel barrels lined up next to the plane in Eureka

to the hangar, so it would be ready to load quickly should the weather hold overnight. After a final call home, I attempted to get some sleep, but it was impossible. At 5 a.m., I called the hangar and received good news: we were flying. Anxious, we dressed and headed over to the airport. It was clear and bitter cold, and it bored into our cores; the thermometer said it was minus 30 degrees. As we loaded up our gear, Terry the pilot, whom I had met in Antarctica, looked at us and said, "You guys got a lot of gear." I told him I was sorry, but he just shrugged and said, "That's OK." The Norwegians were all smiles as they loaded up their smaller sleds. The four of us crammed into the back of the barely heated De Havilland Twin Otter, each man trying to stay warm. As the plane lifted off, I was torn between two emotions. The first was elation that we are finally off. The other was trepidation at the thought of leaving the luxury of civilization for nearly two months of incredible hardships. But then I looked out the

Overleaf: Heading north from Eureka to the Discovery Ice Rise

Looking down at the Discovery Ice Rise, where the smooth snow stops and things get rough—that's the Arctic Ocean

window and saw the most amazing sight. On one side of the plane the full moon was setting, and on the other the sun was rising. It was stunning. Both the sky and snow were the blue of Arctic twilight, and as the sun rose slowly, it revealed a blank landscape as far as the eye could see.

It took us two and a half hours to get to Eureka, which is 390 miles north. When the plane touched down, we could feel the bitterness of the Arctic though the windows. It must have been at least minus 45 out there. While the pilots filled the tanks, both Ryan and I kept swinging our arms and running around; anything to stay warm. When the temps drop that low, you can start to freeze in all of your gear in minutes if you don't stay active. Luckily, the pilots decided that they didn't need to ferry the two teams separately to Cape Discovery. They could handle the excess weight.

In another hour and a half, we were circling over the Arctic Ocean ice as the pilot looked for a place to land. Peering through the frosty Plexiglas window, I started looking for a path north through the highly fractured and pressured ice. It looked pretty bad. My heart sank, knowing all too well how the ice conditions would impact our expedition. In 2010, we were greeted by large expanses of open water. That was also tough, but I knew that what I was seeing now was a whole different animal. Traveling through it would be brutal. Glancing over at Ryan, I saw he was already filming in anticipation of landing. He flashed me a smile and a quick thumbs-up.

The plane's skis hit hard and bounced off the uneven snowdrifts. We flung forward as the pilot reversed the engines and the plane skidded to a halt. Our weight strained against the seat belts, and for a split second, I wondered if the plane would tip on end. I have flown countless miles in Twin Otters in both the Arctic and Antarctic, and while Kenn Borek's pilots are without equal, anything can happen in these extreme conditions. My pulse slowed and I finally allowed myself to relax. We made it.

● ● ●

Out of all the bad ideas I've ever had, this one has to be the worst one. What the hell was I thinking? I wanted to yell this out loud, but instead I kept it bottled inside. We were making hardly any progress pulling these behemoth sleds. Every step was a struggle, and my muscles felt like they might snap. I didn't know if I could make it another two steps. We had been on the ice for two hours now, fighting to move our sleds forward. It was a battle trying to find decent footing while the sleds knocked us off-balance. There were small respites, however, every 200 meters or so. We parked one of the sleds and headed back for the other. The snowshoe walk back was a small break from the intense pain of pulling, and we enjoyed the few moments of relief not straining under the huge loads.

For the moment, visibility was good, but it wouldn't take much to lose the trail in the low light. To become lost between sleds was a constant fear for both of us. We barely spoke and our conversation was reduced to a few words and grunts. We were both in survival mode, adapting to the situation we found ourselves in. As we slowly worked our way through the

Eric goes through a gap in the ice while crossing a pressure ridge.

seemingly never-ending shattered icescape, I struggled to keep a positive outlook. I always knew that the beginning would be hard, but this was ridiculous. In 2010, when my team and I started, we knocked out over six miles the second day. It seemed like there were actual routes through the ice. Not this time. Granted, it was minus 55 instead of the balmy minus 30 degrees we were dealing with now, but my sled was much lighter—120 pounds—and there were more leads to work with once we got onto the ice. Even then dragging the sled was hard. I thought I knew what I was getting into this time, but I had badly underestimated the effort that was required to move forward through the current ice conditions with a sled that was almost three times the weight on my earlier trips.

As the sun started to drop toward the horizon, I could feel the temperature drop, and I knew it was time to set up our first camp on the ice. It had been a long day and we were worn out. The last thing we wanted on our first day out was setting up camp in the frigid dark. Just moments before, we had been sweating from the effort of sled hauling. Stopped now, the cold crept in rapidly and shelter was a must. Most important was finding a solid multiyear piece of ice upon which to set up camp. The thinner, first-year ice has more of a tendency to fracture apart, or pressure, and the last thing you want to hear inside your tent is the loud cracking of an ice sheet separating. Or worse, to not hear it. In 2010, a 10-foot-wide gap opened up just a few yards behind our tent. Had our tent been pitched above the widening gap, we would have fallen into the ocean and died. Chances of survival in the frigid waters unprotected are zero.

I spotted a nice open patch of multiyear ice where we could set up our first camp. We took off our snowshoes and immediately wrapped our-selves in our expedition down jackets to stay warm. I grabbed the shovel and cleared a small patch of snow to the bare ice, then put in an ice screw to permanently secure the tent. Working together, we pulled out the tent, slid the poles together. It only took us a few minutes to erect it. Ryan ten-sioned the guy lines, then shoveled snow on the windward vestibule while I jumped in to sweep out the tent. This is crucial, because any excess snow, ice, or crystals will turn immediately into water once the stoves are on. Since the nearest dryer is over 600 miles away, and wet clothes or sleeping bags can literally kill you, it is a priority to keep things dry. The two of us cautiously tossed inside our gear from each sled—sleeping pad, cooking items, food, clothing, and electronics. Once offloaded, the sleds were zipped up and the cook for the night—me—went inside to continue setup, careful to keep all of the moisture out of the sleeping area. I shed my down jacket in the vestibule, but it was so cold that I had to light one of the stoves to warm up the tent enough so I could take off the rest of my layers without freezing. This is one of the worst times of the day, when you are out of half your gear in a frozen tent before the stove has started to warm it up. I worked quickly to get out of my bibs and anorak and change into insulated pants, a fleece, and an insulated jacket. My body shivered while I pulled off my socks and change into dry ones, then I pulled on my down booties. Your body is physically exhausted, and all you want to do is relax. But everything here is work, so I immediately started melting snow for water. Water is the top priority every time we camp. We need it to stay hydrated and to make breakfast, lunch, and dinner. I wrapped the heat exchanger around the pot, then my homemade windscreen/support around that, and then I placed the whole set over the stove. I poured a

The team's first dinner on the ice. Note the number of water bottles lined up to be filled.

little water in the pot and then added a few snow chunks. As soon as my shivering stopped, I fired up the second stove and began hanging gear over it to dry. While the heat from the stoves was welcome, one of our main concerns was rationing fuel—if we use too much now for warmth, we might run out before journey's end. I booted up our GPS and checked our progress: only 1.16 miles. Not an impressive first day. Sitting on my sleeping pad, I was barely warm, but the temperature inside was slowly creeping up. While I was inside, Ryan was busy outside. He shoveled snow over every one of the snow flaps to insulate and stabilize the tent. With that task complete, he cut a large pile of snow and placed it in the back vestibule of the tent; that would be our source for water. He recorded a short video that would hopefully be used in our Animal Planet TV show. Once in the vestibule, he rolled up his down jacket and stashed it in the corner, then he took off his parka and brushed the frost out of the ruff. He unzipped the main tent door and lumbered slowly in. I filled up our first water bottle and tossed it to him while he changed into his insulated pants. He hugged the warm water bottle close. As the liquid cooled, he would drink it and we would refill it at bedtime. One of the few luxuries on a polar expedition is having a hot water bottle inside your sleeping bag with you. We would each sleep with two every night, one at our feet and one at our crotch.

I began to prep dinner, and simultaneously tapped out a blog post on the PalmPilot. It's antiquated but it works. It was a pain in the butt typing out one letter at a time with the small stylus on the keyboard in sub-zero temperatures, but Web updates were an important part of telling our story in real time. In between cooking, melting water, and sending out updates, the two of us were drying gear (socks, balaclavas, underlayers, face masks, goggles) on the clothesline hung above the stoves. Dry gear is crucial to success. I looked over at Ryan through the forest of gear.

"Wow, that sucked," he said. Yeah, that pretty much summed up my feelings. It was a brutal day. A little while later, we ate our piping-hot rehydrated meals in silence as both of us reflected on how hard the day had been. It was hard to talk over the roar of the stoves and through the jungle of drying clothes. After all our water bottles were filled, we pulled all the clothes off the drying lines and put them in stuff sacks. I turned off the stoves, capped the fuel bottles (so they wouldn't leak), and then placed the cooking equipment and stoves in the back vestibule. Only once all that was completed could we pull our sleeping bags into the tent.

Even though we had only made it 1.16 nautical miles, we were both still in a good mood. The great adventure had begun and we had survived the first test. Yes, the pressure ridges were bigger than expected, and the sleds were damn heavy. But there was hope. Every day that went by, our loads would lighten. The rotten, shattered ice we were in could not continue for too many days; we were bound to break into some clean leads and floes soon. Our mileage today was surely an aberration. Tomorrow, with a full day on the ice, we would start to put up some better numbers. As we slipped off to sleep, I optimistically hoped tomorrow would be better. It was the last bit of hope I would have for a long while.

I Must Be Nuts

Coordinates: 83 degrees north, 419 miles to North Pole

It was pitch black when I woke up, and for one brief moment I think I am in bed next to Maria back home in Boulder. I must have been dreaming of her. The thought of her next to me lingered while my senses slowly came to. The freezing air filling my lungs and the clammy wetness inside my sleeping bag quickly reminded me where I was: floating on a sheet of ice over the Arctic Ocean, 3,000 miles from home. There was no comfy bed and a beautiful woman in my near future; only endless hours of suffering ahead. Reality is hard here.

Due to the ever-present moisture and cold on the Arctic ice pack, our chosen bedding is both complicated and barely comfortable. We used a relatively simple three-layer system, but each layer served a specific function. On the outside, acting as a first defense against the cold and moisture (frost) buildup, was a Nemo Mezzo Loft synthetic sleeping bag. It is a three-season bag and only rated to 30 degrees, not something you would expect to see in such an extreme environment. It served three critical purposes: provide a layer of insulation from the cold air outside, keep as much moisture, frost, and ice away from my inner sleeping bag as possible, and preserve the loft of the inner down bag throughout the night. Tucked inside it was my second bag, a Nemo Canon down sleeping bag. Rated to minus 40 degrees, I got it sight unseen because it's the perfect bag for this trip, warm as hell, durable, and minimal exposure to the elements. We slept completely cinched up inside our entire sleep system. The only aperture to the outside air was through a small hole around the mouth and nose. Ideally a four-inch-tall chimney rises above your face,

Left: Hoarfrost crystals on the clothesline

which allowed all incoming air to be warmed before you breathe it in; its stovepipe design protects your face from direct exposure to the frigid outside air. At times, it can feel like a coffin. The temperature inside our tent was only a few degrees warmer than outside, so the small breath hole was a weak point in the entire system. If I only had to sleep inside those two bags, bedtime would have been wonderful. But since nothing is simple up here, we had to add one more layer: the dreaded, uncomfortable vapor barrier, which we crawled into and pulled up around our heads at night to prevent body moisture from getting into our sleeping system and freezing solid.

One of the biggest challenges we have once we set up the tent, besides not burning it down, is keeping out gear dry over the entire expedition. The Arctic Ocean ice cap is unlike any other region on the planet. Since only a few feet of ice separate you from the ocean, it is very humid, and there is a lot of moisture in the air that freezes on tent walls and in our sleeping bags and clothes. Unlike in Antarctica, which is technically a desert, or Mount Everest, where the climate and snow are drier due to elevation and where your wet gear can dry out in the wind, sun, or your tent, up here in the Arctic, drying anything without the aid of our small MSR stoves is impossible. Just about everything that got frosty during the day had to be hung and dried over the stoves in the evening. It is a process that requires your full attention. Several times I have ruined gear by being distracted for a minute, only to turn back and see something melting from the heat of the stove. In 2010, I half-destroyed my goggles three-quarters through my trip when I looked away for just one minute. Most of the lens surface was scorched, leaving them barely usable. I tried to ski without them the day after the incident, but not only did my sunglasses freeze, but without the attached nose beak, my face quickly froze as well. I looked pretty humorous to my companions tilting my head down to see out of the small clear band of nonmelted lens. Hanging socks and gloves over the flame is challenging as well, but at least they are small

> While you sleep, your body will give off close to a half-cup of perspiration.

and easily manageable, and we use safety pins to ensure that wind or our movements don't knock them into the flames only 12 inches below. However, attempting to dry out a sleeping bag on any given night would be impossible. We simply don't have enough fuel to melt and dry even one night's worth of accumulated frost, plus the chance of burning holes in them is too great.

While you sleep, your body will give off close to a half-cup of perspiration, plus each breath you exhale is also loaded with vapor. The only way to keep that moisture from soaking the down in your sleeping bags is to funnel your breath out of your bag (hence the stovepipe design of my bag) and to crawl inside of a vapor barrier every night. The vapor barrier is a liner that goes between you and your bag and cinches up, so the only thing free is your face. It is made out of waterproof Sil-Coat nylon to keep all of your moisture in. The best way I can describe it is that it's like sleeping in a wet plastic sack. It's really uncomfortable and can cause issues on long trips when cuts and rashes never get a chance to fully dry out or heal. But the vapor-barrier liner—like all our other gear here—is a valuable component of a bigger system designed to stack the odds ever so slightly in our favor. And with an expedition that spans nearly two months, we didn't have the luxury of not sleeping. So if I had to sleep inside a clammy wet plastic sack to stay warm and safe and hopefully reach the North Pole, then so be it. Quick note here: In Arctic conditions, it is often too cold to get up at night to go to the bathroom, so you sleep with a Nalgene bottle to pee in at night that you dump out each morning. Sounds gross, but it is better than going out into subzero temperatures several times a night to answer nature's call.

I carefully loosened the enclosure around my face and looked around; it was pitch black out. With the polar winter ending, we would have just six hours of light for traveling; it's just too difficult to travel at night. As each day of our expedition passed, we would gain about eight minutes of sunlight, until we would be crawling in the tents while the sun was still

Overleaf: The first morning on the ice, Eric and Ryan try to "dry" their sleeping bags on the sleds before heading out.

up. More light means warmer temperatures and longer daylight hours to travel on the ice. At this point, we needed to be heading north as the sun rose above the horizon, because every minute is precious. So we began our morning routine four hours before we planned on heading out.

I unzipped my sleeping bag and slipped one hand out to reach over and nudge Ryan awake. His muffled reply let me know he was awake also. Looking around the tent in the beam of my headlamp, I could see that every surface is covered in a half-inch of hoarfrost crystals[1] that glisten in the light. It looked like the inside of a freezer; every movement caused it to snow inside the tent. It must be close to minus 30 degrees. I grabbed the tent brush next to my head and started to sweep off all the surfaces around me, careful not to let any of the crystals get inside my bag. After the tent walls, doors, and clothesline were swept clear, I turned to my sleeping bag.

> The Arctic Ocean is easily one of the harshest environments on the planet, and it literally destroys gear.

Once all of the frosty detritus was brushed outside the tent, both of us got out of our sleeping bags. I slept in all of my baselayers and kept my insulated pants down around my ankles close at hand as a safety measure, in case the ice cracked underneath our tent and I needed to escape quickly.

Rapidly, we pulled on our lightweight down sweaters and booties. It was damn cold. My teeth were chattering, and the fog from my breath swirled in front of my eyes. Out went the sleeping bags into the vestibule, inside the bivy sacks to keep them dry. We did this as quickly as possible, and then we dove back in the tent to get both stoves lit as fast as we could. Whenever the stoves were running, the bags were outside. We couldn't have them inside, because as soon as we light the stoves, any dampness in them—it's impossible to keep them perfectly dry—will sink in and they will become big ice cubes. Fumbling with the first stove with numb fingers was very painful and miserable, but then the first one sparked and the dim blue light of the burning gas illuminated the tent and warmth began to spread. Soon the temperature in the tent would be somewhat bearable, reaching as high as 30 or 40 degrees. When we lit that stove, we felt like civilized human beings again, as we time warp from Neanderthals huddling in a cave to modern *Homo sapiens* capable of complex thoughts. Still, it took several minutes for the heat radiating from the small burner to melt away most of the pain and discomfort.

Once the temperature in the tent was bearable, I began the water-melting process again; it's a constant task, and we needed to replenish any liquid we drank in the night, rehydrate our breakfast meals, and make soup and drinking water for the day ahead. On the other side of the tent, Ryan was looking over his gear to check for any damage. The Arctic Ocean is easily one of the harshest environments on the planet, and it literally destroys gear. At minus 30 or 40, nylon tears like a sheet of paper, tent poles snap like dry twigs, and plastic fractures and cracks when touched. A broken zipper, a leaky fuel line, a tear in a sleeping bag—any could spell disaster not only for our success, but also our survival.

While the snow melted, I took my turn on the satellite phone to make an audio update. Part of our morning ritual was to call in and leave an update on our website, so that people back home could follow our expedition live. I chose to do these in the morning, because in the Arctic I'm just so worn down in the evening that it can be hard to find anything good to say about the day that has just passed. After some sleep I am usually able to look at the prior day's events with a modicum of positivity. Still, there are many audio updates on my website where you can hear the philosophical weight of the expedition and the internal struggles that are going on when I call in. Today's update was tough. Besides the brutal ice conditions, I was already missing my family.

My breakfast was like all of my other meals: reconstituted Mountain House freeze-dried dinner mixed with 20 grams of butter. While Ryan opted for an oatmeal-granola mix, I find that I like savory foods more than sweet and, after a lifetime of eating leftovers while I'm at home, I decided to do the same for breakfast. Size-wise, each breakfast was roughly one-and-a-half pouches of a normal dinner (spaghetti, beef stew,

Overleaf: Making breakfast in the tent

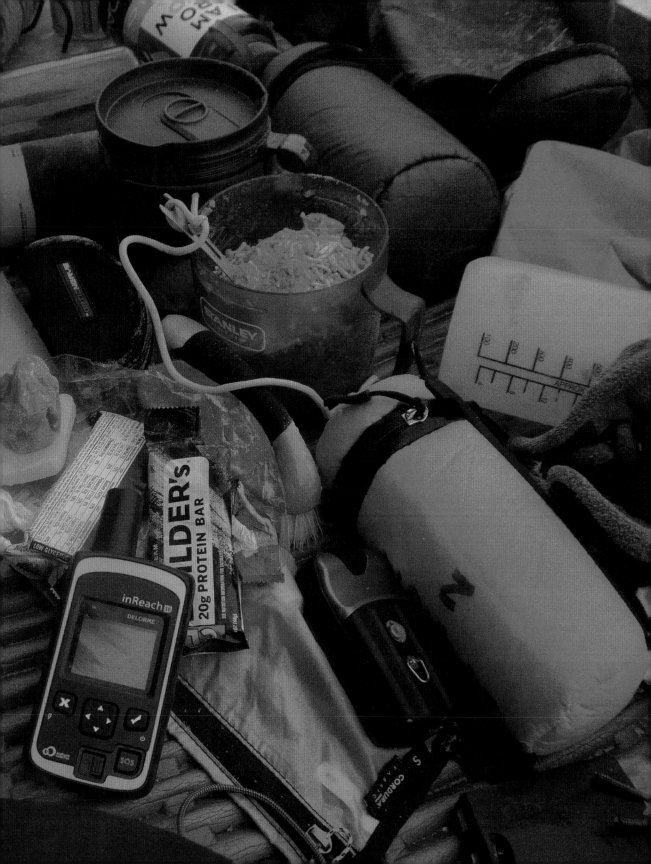

beef stroganoff, etc.). Each pouch contains roughly two to three servings. That means for breakfast I was eating about four servings, and dinner was close to six. Of course, my calorie consumption didn't end there. We supplemented all our meals with butter and olive oil to add extra fat and increase our overall calories.

While I ate, I pulled out my iPhone to look at pictures of Merritt and Maria. I saw that the charge was already getting low, so I opened up my gear bag to pull out the charging cord. That's when my world fell apart.

I feel tears come to my eyes as I dig through my gear, frantically looking for the cord. I couldn't find it. I must have left it behind. How could I be so stupid? I had preloaded a ton of photos of Maria and Merritt before we left, plus hours of podcasts, audiobooks, and music. This was my link with home, and the thought of soon not having the ability to access it crushed me. Ryan's phone was an older model, so his cord would not work with mine. As I turned off my phone to conserve the battery, my mind sank into depression. I knew all too well the cumulative mental toll of this type of travel. With no distractions and no connection to my family, there would be no break from this icy hell. I would surely crack. How would I be able to continue? What the hell am I doing here?

> How would I be able to continue? What the hell am I doing here?

I broke down in front of Ryan. He was supportive but not overly compassionate. I appreciated his kind words, but didn't blame him for his apparent lack of empathy. He was dealing with his own issues. I knew he was feeling overwhelmed already; this was unlike anything he had ever attempted before. The previous night, when we were discussing the day, he said to me, "I feel like I am back in kindergarten. All of my prior experiences mean nothing out here." I was sympathetic to his feelings. There really is no way to prepare for the challenges that will be experienced on this trip. It's that unique. All you can do is keep heading north and deal with issues as they pop up. But our combined success must first come from inside each of us individually, and mentally preparing for inevitable stress, discomfort, and fear of the day ahead takes all of our focus. There was not a lot of talking in the tent after we woke up.

After breakfast, while I filled our thermoses with hot soup for lunch and water mixed with electrolyte drink mix for the day ahead on the ice, Ryan geared up and headed outside to start packing up his sled, remove the snow off the tent's snow flaps, and get the snowshoes or skis out. I shut down the stove and packed up all of our inside gear. I had already changed out of my insulated pants and down sweater and into my expedition bibs during my last few bites of breakfast. Time is of the essence here. The longer I took, the more time Ryan would have to stand around waiting for me. It was minus 20 outside, and hypothermia or frostbite can set in in a matter of minutes, so our carefully choreographed system of dressing and packing up gear and camp was designed to save both time and our lives. I tossed all of my gear outside and started to load my sled up while Ryan started to prep the tent to come down. The two of us had to run around in a circle for 10 minutes to get our blood flowing before we felt warm enough to drop the tent. Every single task made us painfully cold. Using fingers and hands at this temperature to zip, pack, and shovel is quite simply miserable. Together we rolled the tent up carefully and efficiently; it is our home, critical to keeping us alive. We couldn't afford to damage it. As I zipped up the cover on my sled, I noticed a small tear on the top. There was nothing I could do now except hope it wouldn't get any bigger before I could fix it at night.

Clipping into the harness, I looked at the compass hanging around my neck to align us with north. I could still see the looming mountains of Ellesmere Island behind us, so it wasn't that difficult to figure out which direction to go. But later on navigation would be impossible without our compasses. I noticed there was a slight dusting of fresh snow all around us. This was not good: it will slow us even more. At this temperature, there is very little moisture in the snow, and the intricate ice crystals (since they had not been knocked down by the wind yet) would act like sandpaper on the bottom of our sleds, providing yet another obstacle to achieving our goal.

Overleaf: Clipping in to one of the sleds, looking back south

Wrapped up from the cold. Leaving one small part of the skin exposed is dangerous in the Arctic.

Leaning forward, I gripped my poles so tightly I could feel the circulation cutting off to my fingers. It took us three attempts to get the sleds moving. After just a few minutes, we hit our first pressure ridge—which, thankfully, wasn't that big. Still, our sleds were impossibly heavy, and it didn't take much of an incline to reduce our pace to a crawl. Each pressure ridge is different and requires a different strategy to traverse. This time, we both heaved the front of Ryan's sled up onto an ice chunk, and then pulled it over. Once at the crest, Ryan braced himself near the back of the sled to ensure it wouldn't get out of control coming down. Ahead of me was a quagmire of ice. There were huge chunks of older pack ice jutting up in all directions. I aimed us for a gap between two huge blocks ahead of us. A few steps in, Ryan fell through a gap in the snow, his leg sunk to his crotch. I didn't see this happen, as I was a few feet in front of him, but the sudden addition of weight on my line alerted me that something was wrong. It was hard to see anything except what's in front of me, my whole world reduced to the small opening in my parka hood and fur ruff. Underneath my head was wrapped in a neck gaiter, stocking cap, and a full balaclava. With the addition of my goggles and nose beak, no single part of my skin is exposed to the frigid air. Consequently, it is very hard to hear anything. When the wind is blowing, as it often does, you have to holler out loud for someone standing next to you to hear you.

As Ryan pulled himself up, I catch my mind fighting me. *What are you doing here? Just turn around and head back. Are you this selfish to leave your wife and kid behind while you undertake such a dangerous endeavor?* A constant stream of doubts running through my head is normal on every expedition I do. Alone with just your thoughts on the ice—it was still too cold to listen to music, even if I hadn't forgotten my charging cord—as you strain to move forward each step, you are constantly battling your emotions. With no other outside stimulus, very quickly on these types of trips you come directly up against who you are. Any mistakes that you've made, things that you've said, everything that makes you you, good or bad, is right there in front of you, unfiltered—mocking you at times, but always unfailingly there for you to look at, evaluate, and assess. One minute you're on an emotional high, the next in the depths of misery. Pretty quickly you start to see your mistakes and the path that a better version of you would have taken. I took a deep breath and let the self-criticism flow away. I have often said that the only way to succeed is to put yourself in a situation where you don't have any other choices. We just need to keep moving forward, because right now, even giving up is impossible. There is no way a plane could land in this jumbled mess of ice. Our best chance of getting home is to simply keep moving north.

We traveled another 400 feet over the next 15 minutes, continually route-finding and battling bad ice. As we unclipped to head back for my

One minute you're on an emotional high, the next in the depths of misery.

Overleaf: Nothing is easy at minus 40 degrees.

sled, now out of sight, I noticed that the wind had blown our track out. Luckily, I saw some marks ahead, coming through a gap in a pressure ridge. Even though we came this way just a few minutes ago, it was hard to tell one chunk of ice from another. Like old trail-hardened trackers from some Daniel Boone story, we looked for traces of our rapidly disappearing tracks. At some point, I picked out a small hole in the snow made by a ski pole, then the outline of one snowshoe, until we top out on a pile of shattered ice where we can finally see my sled again. It is a huge relief. As we hooked into the ropes, I looked at Ryan, and he said, "This was your idea," with mirth in his voice. I started to laugh immediately at the absurdity of our situation and the futility of our efforts.

When I first met Ryan in 2009, I knew he was an incredibly accomplished mountaineer who was looking for a new challenge. After successfully guiding expeditions to the top some of the most iconic 8,000-meter peaks in the Himalayas—Mount Everest four times, Cho Oyu and Manaslu three times each, Lhotse twice, plus K2, Broad Peak, Gasherbrum, and Dhaulagiri—he had serious credentials. Toss in the several years he spent climbing numerous peaks across the Andes Range in South America and I had full faith that he would be successful in his unsupported trip to the South Pole. When he and his partner, Cecilie Skog, ended up making the longest unsupported traverse of the southernmost continent, I was not at all surprised. When I started to seriously think about heading back to the North Pole in 2012, I knew I wanted him on my team. We had climbed Denali together in 2009. Ryan was the "sensei" and I the "grasshopper" soaking up knowledge the higher we climbed. We had a good rapport, which is actually more important than physical skills on an adventure like this. There is a long history of expeditions failing due to personality clashes.

Ryan is very pragmatic where I am much more emotional, so the two of us balance each other well. I knew that in the early part of the trip, I would be making most of the decisions, because I had the experience

Right: Ryan, a bit frozen

Navigating on the ice

with the unique challenges of the North Pole. But I also knew that as we went on, as he became more comfortable, his experience would prove to be invaluable. He was highly motivated to do the trip in order complete the Explorers Grand Slam. He had already completed the Seven Summits, many of them numerous times, and had bagged the South Pole. If we could make it to the North Pole, he would be only the 10th person to complete this feat. Rarefied company indeed. If I was going to make it back to the pole for a third time, I knew Ryan would be an integral part of it.

As we started to bring my sled forward, my harness was creaking like the rope rigging of an old ship, each tug eliciting a noisy protest. I started to do the math in my head as we battled forward. I had gotten this harness in 2004 for my One World Expedition, and since then it had gone to the South Pole three times and the North Pole twice. All of that time dragging heavy sleds under the extreme cold and harsh ultraviolet rays present in the polar regions had surely damaged the nylon. I had planned on getting new ones for each of us before we left, but it had slipped by the wayside as other more pressing issues continually garnered my attention. It was an oversight on my part, and I had gravely underestimated how a sled weighted by an unsupported trek would impact harness performance. I worried that it would break under the intense strain of the long days ahead, forcing a potential end to our journey.

Once we made our way forward to Ryan's sled, we rested for a few minutes before continuing on with mine, leapfrogging the sleds to save time with clipping and unclipping into them. I ran forward to set up our camcorder to tape us. While we both wanted to reach the North Pole, a huge personal goal for me (and the source of the majority of our funding) was to shoot enough video to make a

The line between comfort and hypothermia is unnervingly narrow.

documentary once we get back. As much of a pain as this would prove, it was a big part of what brought Animal Planet on board and critical to achieving my main mission for this trip—tell the story of this incredible journey and little-understood environment. Stories of climbing Mount Everest are now fairly common, thanks to the large number of climbers on Everest each year and several high-profile tragedies on the mountain. The North Pole, however, has seen exponentially fewer attempts and still even fewer successful expeditions. Because only a small number of first-person accounts of Arctic melting exist, there is a huge disconnect in people's awareness. I hope that we can help change that, because the story of what is happening in the Arctic is really the story of what is happening to our planet. And right now that story is looking pretty frightening. This is an adventure and an environment that may realistically cease to exist in the not-so-distant future, and our Animal Planet film could provide valuable insight into what this place is currently like and thus help better understand future changes. After we dragged our sled by the camera, we stopped while I ran back, stopped the recording, and picked up the camcorder. We tucked it into Ryan's sled and set back off.

Overleaf: Leaving the sled behind to scout a path forward.

Over the next two hours, we entered into a cycle of route-finding and agony, dragging one of the sleds forward, walking back to the other sled, and ferrying it forward. This mind-numbing and physically exhausting work, which is the only way to move our heavy sleds forward across the rugged terrain, meant that we were traveling three miles for every mile we moved toward the North Pole. But that is only how it looks on paper. In reality, we moved at intervals of 200 to 300 yards. Fighting for inches at a staggeringly slow pace.

It was so cold out that when I tried to eat an energy bar while walking between sleds, it was as hard as a rock, and I had to break a piece off and warm it in my mouth before attempting to chew it. Part of our snacks remained uneaten during the first week because of this, but I forced myself to stay diligent about eating. I needed the energy. When we stopped for lunch, it was so cold that we couldn't even sit on our sleds to rest and eat. Instead we stood shivering, gulping down mouthfuls of lukewarm soup. We could only rest for 10 minutes before we were forced to run around to get the blood flowing. The line between comfort and hypothermia is unnervingly narrow.

By the time the sun gets near the horizon, both of us are feeling the effects of the day's efforts. Near my physical limit, all my joints ached as if they've been alternately slammed together and pulled apart—which, in reality, they have. My lower back screams at me, and my hands are half-numb from gripping my trekking poles too tightly. When I sighted a relatively flat section of ice ahead where we could make camp, I wanted to cry out for joy. But we still had to bring the other sled up. Still, the end of the day was a huge relief for both of us. It meant a temporary end to the very real physical pain of traveling. Thirty minutes later, I was outside the tent, shoveling snow on the outside, while Ryan was inside, warming it up. I walked a short distance away and pulled my camera out from deep inside my baselayers to shoot a few photos. Looking around, I was struck by the overwhelming, terrible beauty of this place. It is so stark. But it is also stunning; the mountains of Ellesmere Island near our start point were still clearly visible, but just slightly smaller, and all around us was fractured ice.

As I crawled into the tent, I looked over at Ryan. He already knows what I am about to ask.

He says, "1.18 miles today." That's it. All that six hours dragging those damn sleds over the ice got us was 6,230 feet closer to the pole. I had known the beginning was going to be hard, and we would struggle to make progress. But I never imagined moving this slowly. To make the pole and break the record, we knew we would need to average close to 10 miles a day. We couldn't afford to fall too far behind. Still, we were playing a long game here, and getting discouraged about our daily mileage would be useless. We simply needed to put in time and hope for the best. I sighed and reach for my repair kit. I was going to try and fix my sled cover to keep some of the snow out. During the day the rip grew to almost a foot in length, and Ryan's had torn also. I felt responsible for this; I was the one who suggested that we bring the ultrathin covers with us to conserve weight. Turns out it was a bad idea. Had the temperature been only a few degrees warmer, the fabric would have been fine. But due to the extreme cold, the shifting skis strapped on top of the fabric had been tearing it, leaving dangerous gaps where water or snow could get in and gear could fall out if they flip over.

> Dental floss, I've learned, is as strong as it is light, and I've used it to fix tents, mittens, boots, webbing, and more.

Shivering, I slid dental floss into the eye of a needle. Over the years, I've stopped taking any other type of thread or thicker twine for repairs. Dental floss, I've learned, is as strong as it is light, and I've used it to fix tents, mittens, boots, webbing, and more. I could only hold the needle for a few minutes before my fingers become painfully cold. Over the next 30 minutes, I alternated between sewing the tear closed and diving into the tent to warm up. The hot water bottle tucked inside my baselayers provided a little warmth, helping to stave off hypothermia during the process. When I was finally able to come in for good, Ryan had dinner almost ready and the tent, thankfully, was somewhat warm.

Only a few days out, and already Eric has minor frostbite on his cheeks and nose.

As we ate, Ryan asked me, "How do you think the Norwegians are doing?" This is the worst question in the world; right now we need all of our energy to focus on ourselves, not another group.

"You can't worry about the other teams. They're doing whatever they are doing; it doesn't matter," I told him. It was good advice for him, but also for me. If we started obsessing about others, we could very quickly spiral downward. There was no question in either one of our minds that we were in one of the most dangerous environments on the planet, one that would swallow us up if we did not stay focused.

I always forget how brutal of a transition it is from normal life to an expedition. For the first few days it's always an emotional roller coaster. But compared with every other time I have been out, this time seemed worse—especially since I left my family behind. In the past, I was in a relationship, but not part of a family unit. This time things had changed, and the stakes were much higher. I knew that Maria would be fine (more or less), but missing the next two months of Merritt's life weighed heavily upon me. For Maria, two and a half months were a small blip, but that same time frame represented one-tenth of Merritt's life. I would be missing so many big changes and firsts. When I reached into the small stuff sack I wore under my baselayers to pull out the PalmPilot for the nightly blog update, something finally broke my way: a small, white cord, perfectly coiled—the charging cord for my phone. Without even realizing, I had packed the cord as I originally intended. I hadn't forgotten it after all. I was overjoyed.

Several hours later, the two of us were in the middle of a huge mess of slabs, rubble, and ridges.

Even though I was thousands of miles away, I would still be able to look at pictures of my family. I was still connected to them. As I slipped into sleep, images of Merritt and Maria smiling swirled through my brain, and a smile stretched across my weary face.

Out of a million terrible times you'll have in the Arctic, waking up is one of the worst. Leaving a warm sleeping bag and being forced into the frosty cold is nothing short of torture. Worse, morning means a start to sled hauling, and you know that the road ahead of you is paved with pain. At first the beeping from the alarm on the phone seemed like it was coming from another world, or time for that matter. The phone and the alarm are out of place here; way too civilized for such a primal existence. I promptly hit snooze and dozed back off. Ten minutes later, as it dragged me back to my reality, I wondered what the first explorers of this region would have thought had they come upon us in our high-tech tent. They probably would have marveled at our gear while we did the same at theirs. Then they would have wrapped their coats tight and continued north into the great unknown, like the intrepid badasses they were. But they also struggled at times, just like we were struggling, and that gave me at least a small reason to smile. I remembered a quote from Ernest Shackleton[2]

Overleaf: A moment of good ice, but the fresh snow makes it even harder to pull the sleds

about his time in the Arctic: "Difficulties are just things to overcome, after all." Good advice from a man who endured hardships most people cannot imagine. My aching body and self-doubts were just obstacles in my path, and we just needed to keep moving forward, no matter how slow.

Several hours later, the two of us were in the middle of a huge mess of slabs, rubble, and ridges, trying to find a way forward. It was minus 30 degrees but visibility was good—not a single cloud in the sky, and, thankfully, the frigid cold air blowing down from the mountains on Ellesmere Island was absent. My face mask is coated in a layer of ice, and the fur ruff surrounding my face is frosted white from my frozen breath. For the past 20 minutes, we had been pushing, pulling, and quietly cursing my sled as we took it up and over a wall of ice. We had no choice; the "valley" we had been following had terminated in a box canyon of shattered multiyear ice. It is infinitely frustrating to reach a dead end like this, but at the same time, it's equally hard to not be amazed in the same labored breath. The forces required to lift blocks of ice weighing several tons each must have been massive. It gives you newfound respect for this place.

I really am not enjoying being here.

As we lower the sled down the other side, I can see a way forward. But from this high vantage point, the view is spirit-breaking—there is no end to the topsy-turvy landscape we are mired in. We will be lucky to break free anytime soon. As the sled hits the bottom of the slope, we can relax for a minute before we head back for the other sled.

We hear the noise before we see it; then Ryan points toward the sky, and I turn to look in the direction of his extended arm. The red outline of a Kenn Borek plane is in the distance, approaching us as it heads farther out onto the ice. It must be a supply drop for the Irish team; they have been out for almost two weeks now, and their position is much farther west than our current location. Our unsupported expedition means there won't be any supply drops coming for us, but seeing the plane reminds me that there are other people on this planet, and it's not just the two of us. It's something that can be easy to forget out here.

Later that night, while I was melting water in the tent, my mind wandered back to the plane. It would be so easy to get out of here; one quick call, and soon we would be headed back home. Maria would give me a hug and a kiss, and Merritt would melt my heart as we'd run around in the yard. All of this suffering would be done. I really am not enjoying being here. It's just so hard. The day had been brutal, by far one of the hardest I have ever had in 20-odd years of adventuring. The ice never offered us one break; all it served up was a constant diet of crappy, fractured terrain. We made it farther than we had the past two days, 1.68 miles, but that's hardly a speck in our overall goal. We still needed to cover 413 miles, and the clock was ticking. Our drop-dead date for pickup by Kenn Borek is May 4. After that the ice is just too unstable and the pilots won't risk a landing. If we don't pick up the pace soon, our expedition will be over whether we reach the pole or not. While not breaking the speed record would be disappointing, worse would be be skiing for 50 days and not getting to 90 degrees north.

That said, I knew things would get better the farther away from land we got. I had to continually remind myself of the fact. We knew things would be slow at the beginning; they always are. Once we got far enough away from the shoreline, the fractured ice and incessant pressure ridges would thin out. Larger sheets and pans of multiyear ice would be there, plus fresh leads would allow us to make up time. With any luck, the currents would also provide a boost and push the

There are certain things that only someone who has been on an expedition like this can understand.

ice north toward our goal, providing us with a natural moving walkway. Plus the days would get longer. At the moment we were in the coldest part of the trip, when the days are shortest with the heaviest loads, but slowly that would change. Soon there would be more daylight than we would know what to do with, and if we didn't die first, our sleds would become slightly more manageable as we ate our way through our food and burned our fuel. Put in our time: that's what I kept telling myself. I didn't know if I believed it, but I knew we just had to keep moving forward and give it our best shot.

The morning of day four dawned as all the others had. A tent filled with hoarfrost crystals, bodies that hurt all over, a feeling of hopelessness, and temps hovering around minus 30. As the day wore on I wondered how Will Steger, a hero of mine, felt when he led the first unsupported dogsled expedition to the pole in 1986. It was a much, much colder climate then. Temperatures routinely hit minus 70. He and his team were on the ice 55 days and chopped their way through pressure ridges with pickaxes, while navigating by sextant instead of GPS. It was an epic adventure that inspired me in my youth when I was mushing dogs in the Minnesotan wilderness. Will's expeditions still stand as some of the greatest in adventure history, and, surprisingly, he has become an acquaintance of mine, exchanging stories over beers. There are certain things that only someone who has been on an expedition like this can understand. And like me, having seen the effects of climate change firsthand, he has dedicated his life to educating people about global warming. Not surprising to anyone that knows him, Will is still out on winter expeditions even though he is over 70 years old.

"I almost just tore my finger off," Ryan yelled at me over the wind.

"What did you say?" I replied. He crawled down the huge pressure ridge we had just summited, it was nearly twice as tall as him, easily 12 feet high.

"I, er, my finger almost got torn off lowering the sled," his murky reply came from under his face mask. He took off his glove and shook out his fingers; surprised it was still there. It had been a brutal day of double-pulls, each of us pinballing off each other as we stumbled forward, dragging the sleds. Several times we barely escaped a sled sliding into the back of our legs in an attempt to cripple us. They seemed at times to have a malevolent intent about them; each time one would bog down, negative thoughts would flood my mind. When we encountered the massive pressure ridge that we had just dragged the sled up and over, we knew we were close to the end of the day. Twilight was fast approaching, and both

Dragging one of the sleds through a particularly nasty stretch of ice.

of us were worn out. It had been a frustrating day of traversing monstrous drifts and diverting way off course around ridges we simply could not go over. Each time we were stymied, precious time was wasted while we looked for an opening. By the time we ran into this final barrier, both of us had had enough.

I climbed quickly to the top and saw that it was relatively clear on the other side, and in the distance was a potential spot to camp. We made a quick plan to get my sled through by muscling it to the top, then rigging a simple belay to lower it down. It was too dangerous to try to lower it by hand—if it slipped free of our grasp, the sled could shatter, gear could get crushed, or one of us could get injured. Since I was already in the lead, I guided the sled through the rubble, heaving the front of the sled off of ice chunks whenever it got stuck. Ryan is bigger than me, and his job was to lower the sled down while I guided it through. Halfway down, his fingers got caught up in the rope, and the pressure started to crush his finger, slowly pulling it out of joint. Luckily he was able to free it at the last moment without causing any permanent damage, but it highlighted how close to the edge we continually were. Nothing about this place wants us here.

Once we set up the tent, Ryan started to melt the water while I finished prepping the campsite and making snow blocks to melt for drinking water. "I'm freezing, it's so cold out there," I said to Ryan as I crawled into the tent. I spent almost an hour working in the cold, sewing up our sled covers; it is obvious now that they are not up to the task at hand. The fabric is just too thin, and the skis strapped on top just keep tearing it. This is a big issue, due to the fact that as we progress farther in, we are going to be crossing gaps in the ice where the sleds might tip sideways as they pass over. Without functioning covers, we could lighten our load the worst way possible—by dropping gear into the ocean. Plus, if we have to cross open water by swimming in our drysuits, the sleds can dip under the surface as they enter and exit from the ice and the last thing we need is a sled full of water due to a torn sled cover. When I typed our blog post, I decided to keep this fact out. Too much effort describing it, plus there is no reason to worry

> One of the consistent facts of traveling in extreme climates is that it is brutal on your gear.

the folks back home. One of the consistent facts of traveling in extreme climates is that it is brutal on your gear. In just a few days of being out here, I had already broken my camera tripod—the legs just snapped due to the cold. Ryan has been struggling with a ski binding, and my harness sounds like it is going to blow up at any minute. You deal with things as they pop up and make the best of it.

My audio update sent out that night shows some of the frustration and hopelessness we were feeling:

Hey, this Eric calling in at the end of day four. LTD, we are living the dream, Arctic Ocean–style! Ryan Waters is lying down using a Granite Gear model insulator as a pillow in between filling hot water bottles, basically, most of our drinking water for tomorrow, we still have to melt snow in the morning. Anyway, uh, it was a tough day. I wrote a blog post about it. But what I really wanted to talk about today is just the ice, even though it's really difficult out here. I mean, Ryan said today was the hardest thing he's ever done. But the ice today was incredible, which was one of the reasons why it was so difficult. We're on this big section of older multiyear ice that's just been wrapped and smashed together, and you see these huge blocks just heaved up at a 45-degree angle. And you see this really sharp fracture zone, where you can see into that kind of blue aquamarine—just solid, solid ice, and it's just wrapped in all different kinds of shapes and sizes. And then because it's older ice, it's drifted in and so difficult to travel through of course. But I think just seeing the force of nature that it takes to move this stuff and to pile it—you know, five, six, ten, fifteen feet high—I mean it's just incredible. And that's the thought that I would like to leave with you today. If you want to hear about positive things in our actual travel day, well it doesn't really exist . . . Until next time, thanks so much for tuning in.

● ● ●

Why am I here? The question kept swirling around in my head as I lay in my sleeping bag on the morning of day 6. The alarm had just woken me, and my body was slowly but surely rolling out a litany of complaints. On top of that, our encounter with the two polar bears yesterday had gotten me thinking: What would have happened if I had not turned around in time and they had attacked us? This was not my first run-in with a polar bear. Anytime you visit this region, chances are high you will see a few. They are the primary terrestrial predator up here. So why was I upset? I think it must be the fact that everything is so overwhelming; the sense of hopelessness is ever prevalent. In five full days on the ice, we had encountered nothing but hardship and a maze that seems unending. Both of us had luckily avoided injury, but I wondered how much longer the odds would remain in our favor. As the de facto leader of the trip, the pressures of route-finding, decision-making, and worries at our slow progress were weighing heavily upon me. I also knew that the rapid decimation of the ice pack due to global warming means this is almost certainly my last chance to do a trip like this. We raised over $200,000 and, thus far, all we had to show for it is eight miles of actual progress. The mountains of Ellesmere Island are still clearly visible behind us. I miss my family terribly, more than I thought possible. And if the feeling was this strong now, how much worse would it be on day 14, or 40 for that matter?

> In five full days on the ice, we had encountered nothing but hardship and a maze that seems unending.

When I was in Antarctica last year, Merritt was just born and the realities of fatherhood had not yet sunk in. Things are so different now. When I left him at the airport this time, he told me bye and hugged me. Maria and I had been arguing before we left Resolute, and that was weighing on my mind also. What sort of partner am I to leave her alone to run her own business and corral a precocious little boy? I think back to what Lonnie Dupre said to me when he scrubbed our first attempt at the North Pole in 2005: "When will it ever be enough for you, Eric?" I didn't have any answers, but I was hoping that this journey might provide some insight.

After a few hours out on the ice, we stopped for lunch, tucked behind a massive chunk of ice. Sipping my soup, I looked over at Ryan. He is the perfect partner on the ice for me. My mood swings and loneliness don't seem to affect him much. Instead he just puts his head down and keeps plowing forward.

"This is the hardest damn thing I have ever done," he told me. "It is so much different than Antarctica. Nothing is static, and everything is

Eric (left) and Ryan take a much needed break.

changing." I agreed, but as hard as it is, I am OK with the conditions. While all this is new for Ryan, I knew exactly what to expect. This is my third expedition to the North Pole—fourth if you include my failed attempt with Lonnie Dupre in 2005. We talked for a few more minutes, and I assured him it will get better before packing up and heading out. The soup and chocolate were nourishing. It helped to replenish both our bodies and our spirits.

One hour later, I just want to toss down my gear and go home. Coming down a rise, Ryan's sled tilted over and a large gash appeared on the top of it, spilling some of his gear. We sewed it up, but had to stop several times in the process to run around in circles, swinging our arms to keep the blood flowing. After that, we started out only to have Ryan's harness shoulder strap break right where it attaches to the hip. The stitching just blew out from the forces being exerted on it. Remarkably, there was

Overleaf: Whiteout conditions

enough excess webbing hanging off that he was able to tie it in, and we were able to continue forward.

The clouds rolled in, turning the light completely flat and obliterating any modicum of surface detail. A whiteout; the worst. When you are surrounded by only one color—white—it can be very hard to see a hole right in front of you. My polarized goggles helped some, but conditions can get so bad that I have walked right into snowbanks or fallen by stepping off ice edges that I couldn't see were there. Keeping momentum on the sled can require all of your attention; the effort of getting it moving can be excruciating. Add in the already terrible footing and the loss of visibility on the ice and things get bad quickly. I couldn't even see the large chunk of ice we were aiming for moments before the clouds covered the sun. I knew it was there but just could not see it. I slipped and fell down for the thousandth time that day, banging my shin on some unseen ice. I didn't think I wanted to go on. It was a low point in a sea of low points.

> Sometimes you just have to put one foot in front of the other and things work themselves out.

But, as is starting to be the dynamic out here, when one of us starts feeling discouraged, the other keeps it positive. It seems like such a small thing, but it provides just enough boost to get us through.

"Let's just start moving toward that close chunk of ice and we'll figure the next steps as we go," Ryan suggested. Each step was a chore, but Ryan was right. We figured it out and soon we were in our tent. Sometimes you just have to put one foot in front of the other and things work themselves out.

In the tent that night, we received news that both the Norwegian and Irish teams had been evacuated out two days earlier, when we saw the plane. The Norwegians had frostbite on all 20 of their toes, which I think may have started when we refueled in Eureka. It was so cold that at the time I felt I could have gotten frostbite on my toes. They had stood there while we ran around. When we got back on the plane, I had

Ryan after a few hours on the ice

to take my boots off and physically massage my toes to bring back the warmth—had I not done that, I would have surely gotten frostbite. The two Irish teammates were injured by a sled falling on them as they lifted it over a pressure ridge. It reminded me of how one simple mistake can doom an expedition. While I felt bad for the Norwegians, an unseen burden was lifted from our shoulders. We no longer felt that we were locked in a race against another team. Additionally, there was a small solace in knowing that other people were on the ice and it was hard. So hard, in fact, that now there were only two teams left on the ice, Yasu Ogita and us. I hoped he was doing well. As we settled in for the night, I looked over the video I had shot a couple of hours earlier, right after we had set up camp. We had not been filming enough so far; the struggle for survival had taken precedence. In the video, you can see that my emotions are barely under control. Several times that day I had been reduced to tears.

It's the end of day six. And it is so incredibly cold right now. It's colder than you can even possibly imagine, and this has probably been the hardest six days, easily, of my entire life. I mean, this is where we've, we've gone like one mile a day, basically. Maybe a little more. Our sleds are so incredibly heavy . . . that we have to both of us haul our sled together and then go back and get the other one . . . We're just not making any miles and we don't have a lot of time overall. I mean, 50 days seems like a lot of time, but it's not. And we're going really slow . . . It's such a physical and emotional roller-coaster because just trying to remain positive and optimistic when you're just surrounded by just the worst conditions possible. And just standing is an effort of survival, let alone trying to move through the environment and stay upright and eat and sleep, and everything is just difficult. To make matters worse, we were doing a haul, er, two days ago or yesterday maybe, yesterday, day five—and I don't even know what day of the week that is, on number days it's day five of our trip. We don't really have another life; this is our life: ice, snow, and really damn cold weather. Well anyway, we were doing a haul and we turned around and lo and behold, there's two polar bears there. They had been following our trail—shit it's cold— they had been following our trail for about 200 yards, and right away got the flare out. And I shot a flare off and they just kept walking. Ryan shot another flare off, they kept walk- ing. Finally I had to go get the gun. It was nerve-wracking. I mean, they weren't too, er, worried about, you know, whether or not we were, you know, we were scared. There was a mom and a cub, and polar bears are incredible animals. But if I ever see another one, it will be way too soon, but I just think

> We don't really have another life; this is our life: ice, snow, and really damn cold weather.

the coincidence of the moment that we just happen to turn around. I mean we'd, just we're like, Oh let's go get the other sled, and there they were right in our tracks. Pretty scary moment. But you, you know every moment out here is scary, you just can't think about it. I think on day two I thought I forgot my charger, er, for my phone, and that's got all my pictures of Merritt on it, and that was probably one of the most difficult moments that I've had, because to think about being out here and not being able to look at Merritt . . . was just too much and, and it's just overwhelming. And, and it's already overwhelming enough and basically [*laughs*] I'm like crying every five minutes because it's so hard and scary and everything else. But I am literally getting pummeled by spindrift right now. I'm freezing. It's got to be at least 40 below right now, probably 55 below with the windchill, so staying out here and doing this video is a little too much for me. Thank you very much, have a great day.

Over breakfast the next morning, Ryan and I discussed our options. We were not going to have any chance at breaking the record or reaching the pole if we did not speed up. Something had to change. We knew we could not drop supplies and had no idea when the ice might open up, but double-pulling the sleds was killing us both physically and mentally. After the low point of yesterday, both of us were willing to try anything different. "Let's split the loads. That way we are both pulling our own sleds forward. We still will be traveling the same route three times but at least we are not banging into each other," I said. Ryan agreed, I knew he was just as sick of double-pulling as I was. Any change would be an improvement. Instead of fully loading the sleds and the two of us dragging one forward, we would each pull our own half-loaded sled. Ryan would now be able to take the lead and route-find at times—a huge relief to me—but most importantly, we would not be banging into each other, tripping and falling constantly. Plus the lighter sleds would give our bodies a much needed break. Once we stopped, we would empty the sleds out and head back for the rest of our gear. We were mimicking what we would have done with a four-sled system, but instead of leaving two fully packed sleds when we walked back for the others, we would instead ferry our empty sleds back. It was not the most efficient way of travel, but neither of us could see how it would be any worse than the hell we had just gone through. The main dangers were if we got lost between loads, or having a bear come and ransack our supplies, but those were things we would have

> We were not going to have any chance at breaking the record or reaching the pole if we did not speed up.

to deal with. As we broke down our tent, the cloud cover cleared ever so slightly. It was still overcast and the light was not perfect, but it was an improvement over the day before.

By the end of the day, we had reason to smile: we had knocked out 2.25 miles on the ice, plus we had actually found a pan of ice large enough that we were able to take off our snowshoes and put on skis for the first time since the Discovery Ice Rise.

I turned on our satellite phone to check in with home base. I saw there was an e-mail from Maria. Modern communication systems are wonderful—how else could you be in the middle of nowhere and still able to talk to your loved ones? As I read her words, I was at first elated and then devastated. An innocuous comment about having dinner at some friend's house broke me. At the party, Merritt had called one of my friends Daddy . . . twice. She initially said she didn't want to tell me, but I pressed her over the delayed connection. I wanted to stay an integral part of her life— even on the ice—but hearing my son was calling other men Daddy hurt. I buried my head in my hands and just cried. For his part, Ryan correctly assessed the situation.

"You can't let her tell you that kind of news. It is *not* good," he said. I knew things would be all right, but at that moment all of the demons came flooding back: What the hell am I doing out here, leaving my family behind? What sort of selfish jerk am I to be risking my life like this?

While eating dinner, my mind reeled. I was stuck here. Ryan wisely knew I was struggling and left me alone. What words could he offer me that would help?

It was the wind that first woke me. Even buried in my sleeping bag, I could feel the tent shaking and flapping in loud, random fits. The slapping of the nylon was deafening at times. Sitting up, I looked over at Ryan. He was stirring too. As veterans of numerous expeditions to some of the remotest places on the planet, we're both used to storms. It's a common occurrence. Often the sound of the wind from inside a tent seems much worse than it actually is. So we continued with the morning routines, sweeping frost off our gear, packing up our sleeping bags, and lighting the stoves. The storm seemed to intensify as we ate breakfast, but we still put all of our gear on as if it's a normal travel day. We could not afford any delays, but there was an intensity about this storm that caused a growing concern. Finally, everything was packed, my boots were on and I headed outside: it's a complete whiteout. With no visible horizon, it was like walking into a Ping-Pong ball. I struggled to maintain my balance in the gusts as I checked out the sleds. The snowshoes had blown a few feet away. Quickly I secured them, terrified they will fly away like the house in *The Wizard of Oz*. A quick check of the tent assures me the ice screws are holding, but the side guy-outs have completely blown out. I turned Ryan's sled over and tied in the lines. I pulled my sled to the front of the tent to act as an additional anchor and, equally important, wind block. I crawled back into the tent. "Hopefully it will blow itself out," I said to Ryan. We sit silently, fully dressed, for an hour, hoping for a break in the weather so we can continue. I send in an audio update:

I knew things would be all right, but at that moment all of the demons came flooding back.

Overleaf: Ryan moving forward with sled half loaded when we were splitting the loads.

Hey, this is Eric calling in the morning of . . . day 8, of the Last North Expedition. And, uh, it is blowing . . . pretty bad outside. It's a whiteout, and kind of started the morning off really poorly. We used our sleds to, uh, basically provide a wind block for the tent, and I have mine kind of tipped, angled up so the wind hits more of the bottom of it, perpendicular to the tent. And I just grabbed on a handle and, uh, pulled it, and a couple of the rivets popped out. I know I just kind of like, just going to do it quickly, but, the rivets just broke. Now I gotta fix it. Ugh . . . visibility is just about zero. So really not starting out the day very well at all. Uhm . . . I don't know what else to tell ya. I mean, we're just, we're just out here and making our way and trying to be optimistic and moving forward at the slowest pace possibly imaginable. But, needless to say, Ryan and I are working really well together. I think we balance each other out really nicely. And so having a good team dynamic with each other has been kind of the shining part of this expedition.

An hour later, the storm had gotten exponentially worse; I don't think we will be going anywhere this morning.

Chapter 3

What a Long, Strange Trip It's Been

Coordinates: 83.12 degrees north, 412 miles to North Pole

You sure couldn't tell that it was the second day of spring. Since we woke up, it seemed that the storm only increased in its fury. Both Ryan and I had hoped that it would blow itself out, but that quickly seemed unlikely. The thin nylon shell of our tent was constantly rattling as it was buffeted by sustained gusts of 50-mile-per-hour winds that had lowered the windchill outside to a deadly minus 80 degrees. In conditions like these, exposed skin will frostbite in less than five minutes; all the more reason to love our tent right now. Earlier when I went out to check on our sleds, visibility was nil—15 feet at most—and I almost got blown over. This was one of the worst storms I have ever been in the middle of. It was just nuking out there.

By mid-morning, the two of us realize that we are not going anywhere. The chances of getting lost between loads, or gear just disappearing into the wind and snow, were just too dangerous. Plus, if we took the tent down, we weren't convinced there was any way we could get it back up again without damaging it. "I remember talking with the Norwegians just before we left, and I told them there was no such thing as a 'bad' weather day, you just keep going," I said to Ryan over the roar of the wind inside the tent. "Today I take that back. It's just epic out there, absolutely crazy, there is no way we can travel in this. In all of my years of Arctic travel, I have never, ever, had a weather day where I couldn't move. But today is my first."

Overleaf: Waiting out the storm in full gear, Eric and Ryan have not yet decided to stay put.

As the winds got even stronger, we worried about a strong cross-wind causing one of our tent poles to break. The gusts were so strong, it was causing the entire structure to flex several feet down. But I was exhausted, and fell asleep in minutes. A few hours later, Ryan shook me awake. The storm had gotten worse, so I went outside and buried new guy lines using our Asnes skis and overturned sleds as anchors. Luckily, all of our gear outside the tent was properly stowed; waking up in the morning to a missing snowshoe would most definitely suck.

While getting a day to rest and recover after the beating we've been putting on our bodies sounds good, sitting inside a freezing cold tent won't be too fun. We cannot run our stoves to keep the tent warm; our fuel is strictly rationed to 500 milliliters per day. If we use the stove this afternoon, then no cooking tonight, so no heat. With the temps this low, we can't even listen to our iPhones, because it could damage them. For the next few hours, I got to lie inside my sleeping bag and vapor barrier and try not to go crazy. I try not to let the frustration of a canceled day weigh me

This was one of the worst storms I have ever been in the middle of.

down too much. It certainly is not the first or worst disappointment I have ever had on the ice.

Almost nine years earlier, on May 25, 2005, my heart was broken on my first attempt to reach the North Pole in summer. After 14 days on the ice, Lonnie Dupre and I were forced to stop only 19 miles from our start in Siberia. The conditions were awful. Our mileage was miniscule, and we were constantly drifting backward as the ice moved. We had been planning this trip for three years and had overcome so many obstacles to even get on the ice, so to admit failure after such a short time was devastating. I was furious. Our plan was to cross the entire Arctic ice cap in summer, unsupported, using specially modified canoes. We were each towing roughly the same amount of supplies as Ryan and I were dragging (340 pounds). It was my first-ever polar expedition, and I had dedicated my life to it. From the start it was hard. The ice was shattered and broken, the canoes were cumbersome, and the relationship between Lonnie and myself was strained. We had been at odds since starting out. We were undertaking a huge, untried endeavor, and all of the strains associated with that were at play. Getting on the ice from Russia was a bureaucratic nightmare that taxed our spirits even before we started north. I did not agree with the decision to stop. We had enough supplies for 100 days, and I just wanted to keep going. But I was not the leader, so ultimately I was overruled. Once we waved the white flag, we had to spend nine days sitting on the ice waiting for weather to clear for a helicopter to pick us up. Those were probably the longest nine days of my life.

Once we made it back to Minnesota, and we each had some time to let the wounds heal, the two of us adapted our plan. Heading out through Russia was too tough: there were language barriers, and the permitting was nauseatingly painful. Instead of crossing the cap, we would leave from Canada, head to the North Pole, and then come back. It would be an epic adventure, on par with Richard Weber and Mikhail Malakhov's historic journey in 1995, when they became the first and only team to ever journey to the pole and back, unsupported, from Canada. We teamed up with Greenpeace to promote Project Thin Ice, an initiative that they were launching to put climate change in front of the public. I was excited to be part of something so big. Our blog posts would be widely circulated, and we would be filming to produce a documentary. This was right about the time of Al Gore's movie, *An Inconvenient Truth,* so I had high hopes that we would be able to help make a difference. Almost four years of planning ensured we were prepared. Learning from the lessons of the trip before, we would be receiving a resupply drop, so the canoes were considerably lighter, and we would not get mired in the shore ice.

> Heading out through Russia was too tough: there were language barriers, and the permitting was nauseatingly painful.

Overleaf: This shot was taken only 15 feet from the tent during the storm.

Things started well. The 24-hour cycle of daylight meant we could travel as long as we wanted each day. It was challenging, but right away we were averaging close to five miles a day. It was warm enough that I wore sunglasses and lighter gear. The tents were not an icebox at night, although we still had to sleep inside vapor barriers. Even though the Arctic Ocean is the smallest of the world's five oceans, it still spans 5.4 million square miles—more area than Europe—and being on it for the second time was amazing. I felt sure of myself, since our time on the ice the year before had taught me many of the skills I needed to survive. I was still cognizant of the fact that I was in one of the remotest and most dangerous places on the planet, but as we wove our way forward through the melting pack ice, I felt confident. As I tend to do on all of these trips, I just focused on persevering and moving forward. I knew Lonnie was struggling—the constant strain of working our way forward through the ever shifting ice was tearing him down mentally, plus lugging the sleds in and out of the water had aggravated an old injury in his back. But I had faith we would succeed.

> Without even fully loading our sleds after our resupply, we had cut short what could have been one of the top North Pole expeditions in the history of exploration.

When we received our resupply drop at 86 degrees north, everything fell apart. Lonnie informed me that his back would not hold up to the abuse it was taking, and we were going to stop at the pole. Worse, we would now deliberately slow our pace in order to rendezvous with a Russian icebreaker at the North Pole and, equally important, time our arrival at the pole for maximum media exposure. While things continued to be physically hard and uncertain, the expedition had become something completely different than what we had originally imagined. I wasn't sure if we could make the return trip, but I at least was willing to try. Without even fully loading our sleds after our resupply, we had cut short what could have been one of the top North Pole expeditions in the history of exploration.

I begged him to keep at it. We argued and had heated exchanges. That's when Lonnie, exhausted, asked "When is it ever going to be enough for you, Eric?" I could not answer that. I just knew that I didn't want to give up. We had committed to doing something amazing. Why not try it? It was all to no avail. He was the leader and I was not. For the rest of the trip north I was heartbroken, and our relationship suffered. I remember crying in the tent several times. During those trying times on the ice, I made a vow to come back and try for the pole crossing again. I wanted to do something more classical, more pure to the spirit of exploration. And I wanted to have a good team.

> I am a storyteller, and my goal is to tell the stories of these unique places.

When we reached the pole on July 1, 2006, I was overjoyed. But for years after, I couldn't get the bitter taste of that trip from my mouth. Once we got back, we made the talk-show circuit to publicize what was happening to the ice cap, but the documentary was never made, due to a disagreement between Lonnie and Greenpeace about ownership of the footage. As a result, the story of the Arctic Ocean was left largely untold despite our success.

That is what keeps calling me back to the poles; it is such a unique environment, unlike any other on the planet, yet its story is mostly unknown. Someone stubs a toe on Everest and it's on all of the news channels. But a whole region is quickly disappearing, and you are hard pressed to read about it. I kind of feel like the astronauts must have on the last moon mission: here they were in this amazing place, but people would rather watch *All in the Family.* At the turn of the 19th century when Peary and Cook were battling to claim the first visit to the North Pole, it commanded front-page coverage across the globe. Now, not so much. I am a storyteller, and my goal is to tell the stories of these unique places. After my first visit above the Arctic Circle, I realized that I needed to tell people about the beauty of the poles, something most individuals don't know anything about. Part of these journeys are a form of self-expression, being out in the wilderness and attempting really difficult things, while the other component is to tell a compelling story about a real adventure.

When I finally made it back to Minnesota after that second trip, I was burned out, disconsolate, and disillusioned. It would take me years to fully appreciate what we had accomplished. That trip opened up so many opportunities for me. After a period of time, the idea for the Save the Poles Expedition started to take root in my mind. I would travel to the North and South Poles plus Mount Everest (the third pole) in one year to raise awareness about climate change. It would offer me a chance to accomplish another first in expedition history and a platform to tell my story. While struggling to raise funds for the endeavor, I had an opportunity fall in my lap to guide a trip for Antarctic Logistics and Expeditions to the South Pole. The timing could not have been better; I was a 37-year-old with an empty bank account, living in my friend's basement, in a bad relationship. I was really starting to question the choices in my life and what my future was going to be. In going to Antarctica, I found this community that I'd never had before—people who were interested in the same things that I was. My skills were seen as a really valuable asset there. It gave me a good confidence boost at a time when I had started worrying about my future. I thrived down there. I was able to take that trip and leverage it into some more exposure that helped me start getting companies to listen to my Save the Poles proposal. Plus I actually got paid to go to the South Pole, something that I desperately needed at that point.

In Antarctica, unlike on the Arctic ice sheet, you can actually stop without worrying that you are drifting backward each minute you're still.

The 580-mile South Pole trip took 43 days to complete. It was awesome. Antarctica is a continent, and while you are traversing relatively untouched terrain, the trek has been completed several times previously, so you are following established routes with known dangers. The ice is moving very slowly, and you can ski the whole way. There are no pressure ridges, leads, or thin ice to deal with. Compared with the Arctic, it was like taking a trip to the Bahamas. The sun was out, temps were relatively warm, and I was able to relax. Danger was not lurking around every corner. On polar expeditions, you anxiously tick off each degree of latitude you pass as you head toward the ultimate goal of the pole. The distance between each one is 60 nautical miles—a little more than 69 miles—and crossing each one is cause to celebrate. In Antarctica, unlike on the Arctic ice sheet, you can actually stop without worrying that you are drifting backward each minute you're still.

A few years later, in 2009, I was back guiding another group to the South Pole for Antarctic Logistics and Expeditions and kicking off the first leg of Save the Poles. I led two clients out from Hercules Inlet, traversing over 730 miles to the South Pole in 48 days. Once back, I went into frenzied fund-raising mode for the next two months, trying desperately to secure funds for a North Pole trip. Unlike my first time with Lonnie, I was in charge and had to organize everything. It was nonstop stress going from meeting to meeting, basically begging for sponsorships. I didn't even secure my main sponsor, Bing, until the third week of January, and I was leaving at the end of February. The last five weeks before we left were a blur of minimal sleep, endless tasks, and incessant meetings. I raised nearly $200,000 in two months. Unlike mountaineering expeditions, where $10,000 can mean living like a king in Pakistan for several months, the logistics associated with polar travel are prohibitively expensive. Often it takes years of fund-raising to meet the budget, and for better or worse, much of it materializes in the 11th hour—which adds an additional stress of frenzied purchases immediately prior to departure. After all, what use is $2,500 of freeze-dried food if I'm not able to go?

Anthony Jinman, Darcy St. Laurent, and I stepped off the plane on Ellesmere Island on March 3, 2010, to attempt the North Pole leg of our Save the Poles Expedition. Darcy and I had been planning to do this leg together, and we brought Anthony on at the last minute to complete the team. I knew the hardest part was behind us. We were here; now all we had to do was continue forward. And I would be damned if we did not get there. The beginning was hard; it was much colder, at minus 55 degrees right off the plane, and the ice was all broken up. A full moon cycle had just ended, which is when tidal forces are strongest and the ice sheet moves around much more, creating havoc.

We started out on some big gaps of open water that had just recently frozen over. It was surreal, almost like skiing on the ocean. As we worked our way through the thin ice, I remember wondering where we were going to camp. The ice was too thin to pitch a tent on. Luckily we found one small chunk of multiyear ice where we were able to set up. Normally I'd never camp on anything like that, but one thing you learn to do in the Arctic is adapt to whatever is thrown in your path. Each day the ice got better, and we were making great time. The sleds were only filled with 14 days' worth of supplies, so they weighed significantly less than the ones Ryan and I were pulling. It was still a damn tough trip, but we had the luxury of three resupply drops. Right away we were making over six miles a day, and we were able to sleep eight hours every night and have several rest days. When we reached the pole 51 days later, on April 22, I was excited to celebrate with my team. Little did I know how lucky I was: we were one of four teams to successfully complete the trek that year, and no one else has been able to since then.

> Normally I'd never camp on anything like that, but one thing you learn to do in the Arctic is adapt to whatever is thrown in your path.

When I got back home, Maria was overjoyed for me, but she also knew what was next: Mount Everest. I spent the next few months recovering from both of the poles, regaining my sanity, and trying to organize a trip to Nepal. Luckily Ryan knew a local guide, Tshering Sherpa, a younger man with a soft-spoken, humble manner who would be willing to organize all of the aspects of my climb and summit attempt. His father had been a guide on the mountain who, unfortunately, passed away on its slopes. Ryan thought I was crazy. I was going in the fall, a time when the odds of successfully summiting are notoriously low: only 20 percent of teams make it. The snow and weather are so unpredictable. He told me that there had only been two teams to summit in the fall over the past 10 years, but I was not dissuaded. I had to give it a try. Besides, I didn't have another choice. The spring Everest season was over, and I already had two poles in the bag. I managed to raise $80,000 to get myself to Base Camp at the end of August. As usual, the money trickled in slowly, and there was more than one frantic satellite phone call to sponsors, trying to secure the final funding while I was on the mountain. At Base Camp, there was only our small team and a Japanese climber. Tshering was connected, smart, and careful. Growing up in Nepal's Khumbu Valley, he had seen firsthand the successes and failures of Everest expeditions. For our fall climb, with conditions that would be snowy and colder than the spring, he picked five young climbing Sherpas who he knew would be motivated to make the summit rather than super experienced guys who might not have the same drive. It is substantially harder in the fall due to the small weather window, plus most of the Sherpas had already been up in the spring. By the time we were ready to make a summit bid, it was just the mountain and us, as the Japanese climber, Nobukazu Kuriki, abandoned his attempt shortly after passing Camp III. (He would later lose nine fingers to frostbite on Everest in 2012.)

While it was daunting to be on the mountain alone, it was also the aesthetic that I prefer—like polar expeditions, where it's just you and the ice. Additionally, compared with the lines of hundreds of climbers that Everest sees in the spring, it would be much safer not having to deal with throngs of inexperienced climbers.

But it was also lonely. At a certain point, you just run out of broken English conversations to have with the Sherpas. So I spent my rest days in Base Camp on long hikes down to Gorakshep, the closest village. Still, being on the mountain with no one else there was amazing. I could feel the ghosts of Sir Edmund Hillary and Tenzing Norgay, the first people to achieve the summit, around me as I slowly worked my way up the mountain, and I had the most amazing views all to myself.

I've always said that the best way to be successful is to put yourself in a situation where you don't have any other choice. It's also a very good way to make a life-threatening decision. On Everest, all of my future success was based on a successful summit. While my primary goal was to be safe, I felt an intense drive to continue no matter what. If I didn't summit,

I would be in financial ruin, having borrowed a large chunk of money to reach the third pole. I had everything on the line. Sure, people had been to all these places previously, but I was stringing them together in a single calendar year, and to me that was very compelling. We pushed hard for nearly a month, positioning ourselves for a summit bid, and when we received a good weather report, we put it all on the line, and October 15 reached the summit—and, more importantly, the third pole on our planet. It remains the last successful fall summit of Everest to date.

Sometimes you don't recognize the gifts life gives you until you are able to look back through the mists of time. All my years of guiding, dog-sledding, and living a hardscrabble life had prepared me to stand on top of Everest and at the North Pole for a second time. Without the time I had put in, I could never have made it there. By embarking on my project in 2009–2010, I was able to make it to the North Pole right before the Arctic gods decided to close it down. For the next three years, not one team was able to make it out onto the ice to try for the North Pole. The weather window to fly them in never materialized. Life is funny that way.

When I came home to Boulder and Maria, I was worn out. I had spent nearly six months of the past year in the world's coldest places, living in a tent. The expedition was a huge success, and I received a lot of good coverage. I was able to tell my story, but I also felt like I had left something undone. The documentary I had planned, called *Colder,* never came to fruition as I struggled to pay off the expedition.

Life and my own nature prevailed. I often say that my own worst enemy is myself. I get back from one adventure and start to think about what to do next. Maria is a patient person, but she was ready to put down some roots and start a family. We had moved in together in the fall of 2009, when I moved from Minnesota to Colorado, right before I began the Save the Poles trip. In early 2011, we found out she was pregnant with Merritt. So while I was busy planning the Cycle South Expedition, my next project where I would attempt to cycle to the South Pole on a fat bike, we also were preparing for the arrival of our first child. Through it all, I also knew that I needed to head back to the North Pole one more time.

While I have done expeditions all over the world, there is no place like the North Pole on the planet. It is so unique and so misunderstood. Ask a hundred people what lies at the North Pole and 99 of them will say land. From an expedition perspective, the North Pole has never gotten the attention it deserves.

I wanted to tell the story of the Arctic Ocean: of what this amazing adventure entails. And I wanted to do it in a compelling and heartfelt way. More importantly, I wanted to give a clearer picture of the current state of Arctic Ocean sea ice and how dramatically it has melted since my first North Pole expedition in 2006. In the eight years since I first came here, and area roughly the size of Minnesota and Wisconsin is gone. Imagine if you came home one day and your state was missing. It had just vanished.

Selfishly, I also wanted to test myself and see if I could sustain the physical challenge. The bad taste from 2005 was still in my mouth. We had originally planned that trip to be unsupported, but that changed due to circumstances beyond my control. If I could successfully pull it off, I would join a select group of people: only 47 had ever done it, and this time I would make sure to tell the story about the melting ice sheet.

Over the past century, global temperatures have risen 1.53 degrees[1] and, while that might not seem like much, it is wreaking havoc on the polar regions of our planet— especially the northern pole. Due to their unique characteristics, the ice sheets covering the ocean are melting at a dramatically rapid pace. In the face of ongoing global warming, the poles are warming at a much faster rate than the lower latitudes—twice that of the rest of the globe. It is due to an effect called the ice-albedo feedback, where the melting ice uncovers more of the darker ocean surface below. Unlike the white ice that was covering it before, which reflects almost 90 percent of the sun's radiation, the ocean's surface absorbs almost 90 percent of the radiation. Once absorbed, the water heats up and helps melt more ice. Warm water takes much more time to cool than land does; hence the Arctic Ocean is heating faster than Antarctica. It is a

> Imagine if you came home one day and your state was missing.

vicious circle: the water warms, the ice melts, and that in turn impacts the weather patterns that would normally cool the region. On average, the Arctic ice melt is starting three days earlier each year, a trend that began slowly in the late 1970s but is rapidly accelerating. It's changing that fast. Many scientists predict that we could see an ice-free pole by 2030. Toss in the fact that many of the main ocean currents cool themselves in the north, and you can see why global weather patterns are changing.

The Arctic regions are also the world's thermostat. As the region warms, the permafrost is also melting, releasing a multitude of greenhouse gasses into the atmosphere, only making things worse. Richard Weber has been in the region since 1978, and he describes what he has seen like this:

> From the year 2000 on, the area has undergone a radical change you can see yearly. In the 1980s to 1990s, you would go to the pole and 99 percent of the time you were on old multiyear ice. The route from northern Canada to the North Pole has the oldest ice due to currents, therefore was the most stable. The last time I was there, in 2010, it was completely different. We could walk for days and see almost no multiyear ice. We were struggling to find a safe place to pitch our tents. The temperatures are 30 to 40 degrees warmer than when I first went. It is still cold, but nothing like it used to be.

The first creatures that are feeling the change are the polar bears. They only exist above the Arctic Circle. These denizens of the north are the largest land predators on the earth, and thus require a fair amount of protein. Even though they primarily reside on land, they hunt for food at the edges of the polar ice pack. Anywhere there is a break in the ice, they hunt for ringed seals, bearded seals, walrus, beluga whales, and other mammals. As the pack ice retreats farther and farther from land, they are being forced to travel thousands of miles in search of food. In 2006 we had one approach our tent just south of the pole, looking for dinner. The sight of an emaciated bear is not uncommon these days. Many are starving to death. According to the National Wildlife Federation, the polar bear population has dropped 20 percent in the past 20 years.

Part of what makes the Arctic so vital is that it is loaded with marine life. Seventeen different species of whale can be found there at various times during the year, feeding and giving birth. The abundant phytoplankton in the waters helps feed massive colonies of fish and support the region as one of the main breeding grounds on the planet. As the waters warm, experts are split as to what will happen. The region could crash or adapt. Only time will tell.

A vital part of our existence is disappearing fast. Really fast. That is what brought me back to the North Pole for a third time. I want to tell the story before it is too late.

Lying inside my tent, listening to the wind batter us, it was hard to think about the shrinking ice cap and warming weather. It didn't seem to be happening right now. Every breath that we exhaled was causing crystals to form on everything inside the tent. All that was visible of either of us was our noses. We both fell asleep for some time, then eventually roused for dinner. After a little while, Ryan would start cooking and we would have to abandon our sleeping bags so they don't get wet, but for the moment we hunkered down. As I was starting to doze off, I went over the math in my head: I'm pretty sure that whatever slim chance we had of breaking the speed record is blowing away in this storm. We are already way behind pace and could not afford to lose a whole day. We will just have to adapt to the conditions we are in. To make the pole by the last possible day

> The sight of an emaciated bear is not uncommon these days.

we can be picked up, we will have to average a little more than 11 miles a day moving forward. That is doable, especially if we can break out of the muck and hit some open ice. If the fates are with us, maybe the currents will help us by moving the ice toward the pole, thereby speeding us up, like walking on a moving walkway. Or things could keep getting in our way. Either way, I know one thing for sure: I'm not turning back.

Chapter 4

Better Than a Stick in the Eye

Coordinates: 83.12 degrees north, 412 miles to North Pole

Generally speaking, I am not a morning person. Waking up, for me, is often a painful experience. Waking up when it's minus 30, ensconced in an icy sarcophagus of a sleeping bag, takes it to a whole other level. Waking up in a small tent in the middle of an Arctic blizzard with the wind howling outside is Old Testament brutal, and the prospect of facing another day of pain and suffering can be too much to deal with.

So when my alarm started buzzing next to my head, I did what most sane people would do. I hit the snooze button and dozed back off, hoping to delay the inevitable. One hour later, I cursed myself for giving into temptation—we were already way behind schedule and the last thing we needed was to start sleeping late. There would be plenty of time for that once we made it back home to civilization. As Ryan and I crawled out of our sleeping bags, the mood in the tent was subdued but also somewhat hopeful. While the storm still had us in its grip, we had been able to spend most of the previous day sleeping and recovering from the rigors of the past nine days.

Neither of us had realized how exhausted we were until we were forced to spend the day in the tent. While doing the math in my head, I realized that the chaotic days of planning and packing, plus the delay in Resolute Bay, plus our first nine days on the ice all added up to over two months of mediocre sleep—at best. Although I wasn't waking up at home on a lazy Sunday morning, I felt optimistic as I crawled outside the tent to survey the landscape. It was still a whiteout and the thermometer read minus 30, but I could see farther than a few feet from the tent. I was

Left: The wind and snow quickly bury the team's tracks.

Overleaf: The tent the morning after the storm

The team would leave half of the gear lying on the ice when splitting loads. It was always nerve-wracking.

shocked. The patch of ice that we were on was wind scoured. It was just glare ice. The only snow visible was the small eddies around the sleds and in the lee of the tent. Thankfully we had placed extra screws in the ice yesterday afternoon and set more lines. If not, the tent could have been destroyed. It was the most intense storm I had ever witnessed in nearly 20 years of polar expeditions, and seeing the aftermath, I was relieved that we had decided to stay put. After a few minutes, Ryan joined me outside and we discussed our options. If we stayed put another day, there was a good chance it would be clear the next day. But we would be wasting another precious 24 hours laying inside of the tent.

"I say we go for it," Ryan said from under his hood. "The wind has dropped enough that we can pitch the tent if we're forced to stop. Let's get moving. I can't do another day sitting around." I agreed wholeheartedly. It was time to get moving north again.

As we both hooked into my sled, I was, strangely, in a good mood. We had to revert to double-pulling due to the weather, but it felt good

Eric having fun with his own shadow on top of a pressure ridge. Ryan is out in front.

to be doing something. The decision to not pull half-loads was easy—the weather and wind were too extreme to chance losing any gear between loads. As we started, we were immediately confronted with a maze of jumbled ice, but we slowly picked our way forward. We played a game to see how far we could bring one sled forward before we had to stop to go back and get the other one. We wanted to get a good momentum going, but if we went too far ahead and the weather got worse, we might not be able to find the other sled. Getting lost between loads or losing one sled in conditions like this would mean certain death for us, so we monitored how far we have traversed and noted any unusual formations as reference points.

Over the next few hours, we slowly worked our way through the rubble, only once getting lost heading back for Ryan's sled. For 30 harrowing minutes we struggled to find the trail back, even though his sled was only a quarter-mile behind us. The wind had buried most of our tracks, and the flat light obscured the few that were left. Ryan was having some issues with his goggles, so he stayed in one spot and I walked in ever-larger circles around him, looking for any sign of our passing. Just when the cold was starting to get uncomfortable, I found a single hole poked in the snow from my ski pole. Wandering around hundreds of miles from civilization, I tried to moderate my stress level: this was just another problem in an unending series of problems being tossed in our path.

Toward the second half of the day, we finally ran into the first large pan of ice, some really beautiful multiyear ice free from obstructions, and even better, the wind had scoured all of the snow from it. As far as we could see, there was a clear path—our first since coming down the Discovery Ice Rise on the first day. I looked over at Ryan, and I could tell there was a huge smile under his face mask.

"Shall we switch to skis?" he asked.

"Hell yes," I replied. " I bet we can actually pull our own sleds on this." As we started forward, it was hard but so good. Finally, each of us was pulling our own load on skis. This is what would get us to the pole.

Even though we were floating just over the ocean and there was moisture ever present, the snow itself was very dry. In fact, if we spilled water on the tent floor, we could actually use a block of snow as a sponge—it just soaked the water up. The dryness of the snow often felt like sandpaper underneath our skis and sleds. The fresher the snow, the worse that is. Once the snow has settled, blown, or drifted, the individual snow crystals break, creating more rounded grains, making it easier to travel over. But the daily light snowfall we had been experiencing for the past week had created conditions that were incredibly difficult to pull the sleds over. This patch of clean ice was a more than welcome relief.

Two hours later, we were safely ensconced in the tent and in high spirits. The day had ended well.

"I was really starting to question my decision to come on this trip," Ryan told me over the roar of the stoves. "The ice today showed me we can make it. Hopefully we are breaking free." While it was nice to hear Ryan's optimistic tone, his sentiments made me nervous. If there was one thing my previous time on the ice had taught me, it was this: where there is good ice, bad ice is not far off. Hope is a dangerous thing up here. It's something best left at home. You just need to ride the waves of crap

Ryan takes the lead across the ice.

and keep moving forward. Too much hope can break you. I tried to share Ryan's enthusiasm about the day's conditions, but I couldn't allow myself to feel the same. Tomorrow, I was sure, the conditions would change for the worse.

The next day dawned clear and cold. Both of us were in a good mood, as you can tell from Ryan's audio update.

> Good morning, it's Ryan calling in from the Last North Expedition. So far so good in the morning, getting ready in the tent. We're excited about getting out, and getting onto some clearer ice today, which is really welcome. We finally kind of got out of that initial serious kind of pressure ridges and multiyear, just built-up huge ice, so it looks like for the short term, we've got a little bit of a clear running. Of course, that could change at any point. But it's always good to have a smooth, flat terrain right at the start, so we're expecting

Shuttling loads

to get out and to get good kilometers, miles, nautical miles, whatever you may be following. That's so good for us. Definitely positive, and we're excited about getting down the road a bit. Everything's good with us, we're just kind of finishing up breakfast, finish up water, and we're about to head out in about, probably in 30 minutes, we'll start moving. Early start should be taking the tent down, to start getting after it, so . . . Thanks for following along . . . And we hope you have a great day. See ya.

The pathway ahead was relatively clear as we started out on day 10. Over the next few hours, we were able to alternate between pulling our own sleds individually, splitting loads, and the occasional double-haul. Things were going well, and we were starting to fall into our normal daytime routine. Ryan would lead for the first hour, until we took our first short break. The knowledge that I would be able to eat my first snack (usually a Clif Builder bar) when we switched places drove me forward. Sustenance is a major focus out here. We were burning over 6,000 calories a day at this point, and later, as our energy needs increased due to longer travel days and growing fatigue, that number would rise to roughly 8,000. We had to force ourselves to stick to our eating plans, or the temptation to overeat would result in depleting our food stores to dangerously low levels. Each hour we stop and eat another bar to keep going. We continued to trade off leading until lunchtime, three hours later. By then we were starting to get back into some big pressure ridges, and some of the chunks of ice towering over us were larger than an SUV. It seemed like the perfect place to stop. We like to break for lunch behind a large drift, pressure ridge, or chunk of ice, which can form some semblance of a wind block, but it is more about the idea of protection against the elements than anything else. Huddling behind a piece of ice for warmth is about as ironic as it gets.

Immediately both of us break out our large puffy down jackets to ward off the cold while we dig out our thermoses premixed with some of last night's freeze-dried dinner. The pockets of my jacket are loaded with my ration of salami and cheese, along with chocolate that I greedily dig into. Cold and shivering, I can feel the liquid warming my insides and, more importantly, my soul.

"When I get home, I'm going to go to the movie theater and order the biggest bucket of popcorn they have, along with a slushy, and sit in the theater in a big coat, so I'm warm while I feast," Ryan told me over bites of food. I smiled, and for the rest of lunch I sat quietly, lost in the scene. Popcorn. Chair. Warmth. It sounded wonderful, but before getting too in the daydream, I pushed the thoughts of comfort back down. Our conversations about our "other life" were short and matter-of-fact. We limited them to a few situations. Too much nostalgia about a life we may never see can be as debilitating as a pressure ridge. After 15 minutes, we were back off again. We couldn't afford to linger any longer in minus 30 degrees.

Overleaf: Coming up to a pressure ridge

Over the next two hours, we kept to our routine, trudging forward under the beautiful sky through somewhat-open ice, continually meandering east or west to bypass or surmount obstacles. Every hour we swapped the lead and scarfed down a quick snack; there wasn't much talking between the two of us, both focused on the task at hand.

I was in the lead as we snowshoed through a particularly nasty batch of ice when I stumbled over an uneven piece of rubble. I felt my right knee overextend, and a lightning bolt of pain radiated up through my knee. I almost threw up from the pain. Gingerly, I tried to put weight on it, but every time I bent it, I cried out in pain. Ryan caught up to me and gave me an inquisitive look, I tell him what happened, and he just looked at me, saying nothing. I understood his reaction; both of us were thinking the same thing. If my knee is wrecked, then we're both wrecked, the expedition is over.

Huddling behind a piece of ice for warmth is about as ironic as it gets.

By locking my right leg straight and swinging it around in a modified Frankenstein walk while using my poles as makeshift crutches, I was able to continue on for the next hour. At least once a minute, I was wracked by blinding pain, but I was able to continue forward. Finally, as the sun approached the horizon, we decided to stop for the night. Ryan had not said anything to me while I struggled forward, but I understood. This could be an expedition-ending injury, and at a certain point the best way to be a team is to focus on yourself and do what you need to get through. Surprisingly, once we were in the tent, we realized it was our best day to date. We had traversed 3.3 miles.

Relaxing that evening, the pain subsided. After years of expeditions, both of my knees have issues, and I have been warned that I probably have a partially torn meniscus in my right knee—years of hiking over ice while pulling sleds takes a toll. Hopefully I did not tear it more. As long as I was not putting pressure on it, the discomfort dropped to a dull ache. I'm sure the four Advil I swallowed helped. As we ate dinner, we both agreed that we would keep moving north. I could manage the pain. Hopefully it would die off over the next few days. Painkillers and perseverance would see me through this latest setback. My sights were set firmly on the first day of April, only seven days ahead of us. We would be in a new month, and hopefully the slate would be clean. If I could make it to that goal, I rationalized, things would be fine.

● ● ●

Hey, this is Eric calling in on the morning of day 13 of the Last North Expedition. We've been out here on the Arctic Ocean for nearly two weeks doing just one thing, and that is trying to go north. I don't know if it's been successful or not. We've been nailing away daily just trying to make what seems like an inch of progress. Everything here is a struggle and, uh, just takes a lot of effort and motivation to keep going forward, because it seems like everything is set against us. Did I mention yesterday we've had a little bit of bad luck with gear breaking? My compass broke, which is really frustrating and something that I've never had happen. It was really unforeseen, so we got out the repair kit and epoxied it, and even though there's a slight bubble in it this morning, it should work. Ryan's goggles cracked a long time ago, but he was able to use our spare pair and put his nose beak on, so he was all goggled and nose-beaked up yesterday, which was good; just helps keep the face warm and protected.

Yesterday's ice was a mix of all sorts of stuff. Nothing really good, a lot of drift, and big huge chunks of ice, as well as really huge, massive pressure ridges. If I wouldn't have been hauling such a huge load and struggling with every step, I would have enjoyed yesterday, because the weather was clear and we had good visibility, and the ice was just gorgeous. Just the variety of shapes and forms that exist here are pretty incredible. And at one point, Ryan and I were up on a block of ice scouting the route and the sun was just shining right when our snowshoes kind of moved the snow off the

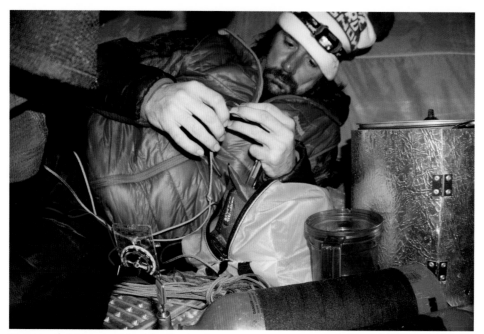

Ryan repairing gear inside the tent

block; you could just see it illuminating, this kind of blue-ish light. It was just gorgeous. Those figurative moments are what really sustain us out here, because when we start looking forward to even next month, it's just overwhelming what we have to do. So we're kind of taking joy in the small things and getting through each day, and in a tent, and eating, and going to sleep again, and waking up, and doing it again the next day.

This morning the weather, the wind pivoted a hundred-eighty degrees, and it was kind of overcast. Hopefully the whiteout isn't too bad, but I'm not that optimistic, unfortunately. I'm a realist out here. But we're still hopeful that we'll have a good day and make some decent miles. Ryan and I have been working really well together, and I take a lot of strength from his just kind of steadfastness and, and, uh, resilience. So that's been really good as our dynamic . . .

The tent, drifted over after a night of wind

Sitting in the tent on the morning of day 13, one thought kept going through my head as I looked back over the past two days. If there is one thing that is certain on the ice, it's this: nothing is certain. Everything is constantly changing, and therefore, nothing will go according to plan. You must constantly be prepared to improvise. If the pathway is blocked, you find a way around. If you're feeling depressed, you find a way to change your mood. If equipment breaks, you fashion a replacement from what's on hand. If the repair doesn't work, you fix it again. If your body is injured, you figure out a way to keep moving forward. The solution is somewhere out there for us to find. But which solution, and in which moment? That's what turns all this into a subjective art form. The moment you stop improvising, or get locked on a certain pathway, you are doomed. When I woke up two days ago in the tent, I had hoped that the pain in my knee wouldn't stop me. Instead of dreading the double-pulls, now I would have to embrace them, because that would give me an opportunity to take a bit of stress off my damaged joint. Instead of

Ryan fights his way through the ice.

walking in full strides, I would hobble along like a crippled robot. But I would keep moving.

Over the past two days, we had somehow managed to creep 6.23 miles closer to the pole. My knee was aching, but I could manage. The 800 milligrams of Advil I was taking every morning helped as well. I could not let something this small force me off the ice. We were lucky to even be here. Since my successful trip in 2010, no one else had made it to the pole by starting from land—not a single person. It's hard to imagine an expedition disappearing completely, but that is the reality we face. The only people that had stood at the pole were tourists and travelers who had paid large amounts of money to travel over the "last degree," from the 89th parallel to the pole. They would fly to the Russian ice camp, spend a week or so traveling to the pole with a guide, then get flown back to the Russian base and fly home. I had decided to call this trip the Last North because I truly believe that this is the last attempt anyone will have to complete this journey. The climate is changing the ice too rapidly. That idea of us probably being the last over-ice expedition weighed heavily on me. Therefore, completing our mission and telling the story of this place were more important than ever.

Richard Weber, one of the preeminent polar explorers of all time and a man who has made the trek seven times, recently had this to say about the conditions up here: "When I first started traveling to the North Pole in 1986, we spent 99 percent of our time on thick sheets of multiyear ice. Very rarely did you run into new ice. During my last over-ice trip in 2010, everything had flipped. There would be days where we would walk all day and struggle to find any multiyear ice. It's much warmer, and there is so much more open water; we never saw this in the 1980s and 1990s. The change has dramatically accelerated since the year 2000, and I believe that within 20 years, you will be able to sail to the pole in the summer. It will be ice-free." Those are pretty scary words from a man who has completed seven over-ice trips to the North Pole.

At lunch two days earlier, Ryan looked over at me and asked, "Have you ever used a Green Egg grill? Man, they're awesome." I laughed so hard, I almost spit out my soup. After battling the ice all morning with only an occasional grunt between us, that is what he chose to discuss. The absurdity of it was perfect for our situation. For the next 10 minutes, while we huddled behind a towering block of ice in the middle of nowhere, the two of us discussed the attributes of different grills and grilling on my back deck. It's the little things like this that keep you going. Instead of discussing the demons both of us are battling—self-doubt, pain, fear, and loneliness—we find something to brighten our moods. It's these kind of moments that are the real gems of our partnership, the times when we are able to just talk about something random and help one another be transported from this place.

The sickening feeling I had yesterday when I looked down at my compass for a bearing and saw a steady stream of air bubbles seeping into

Overleaf: Ryan attempts to navigate through the ice.

Ryan checks the team's heading with the compass. In the Arctic, there are no landmarks to navigate by. Without a compass, they'd be lost.

the previously sealed case was even worse than the pain emanating from my knee. I wasn't even sure how it happened. A tiny fracture in the dial was allowing air inside where the needle is housed. In years of expeditions, I had never broken a compass, and the implications were significant. Our compasses are our eyes. In this beautifully bleak environment, it is impossible to know which way is north. If the sky is perfectly clear, we can still see the fringes of the mountains behind us. We can also use the sun and wind to navigate, but these are constantly changing. Equally important, my compass relieved stress. When it came to making a difficult choice about which way to travel around a pressure ridge or lead, I would bring my compass to level and the needle would point north. Simple solution. A compass is our only option for continuing north in any efficient, reliable manner. Already we were experiencing some issues with Ryan's compass—it had an air bubble caused by the extreme cold. If mine went on the fritz as well, we would be functioning with two very subpar compasses, wasting valuable time wandering in a zigzag pattern instead of staying on course. As we hastily dug through Ryan's sled for the repair kit, the stress got the better of me. "Come on, where the hell is it?" I snapped at him. "Hurry up before it's ruined." I was furious at him, myself, and yet another setback. Finally he produced it, and I rapidly superglued the gap in the plastic and covered it with duct tape. It was minus 30 and nothing seemed to stick, but the bubbles stopped, so I assumed the fix worked. We could keep moving for now, but I would need to find a more permanent solution. Of course, with a large air bubble in my compass, it took longer to get a correct heading. But at least it still worked.

Later that night, we came upon a novel solution to our rapidly disintegrating sled covers. Both of us were tired of the Sisyphean task of sewing them together. We would lash our sleeping pads over the tattered covers to hold our gear in before we headed out. That would protect the covers from being torn further by the skis and snowshoes. When another leg broke off the camera tripod yesterday morning, I managed to fashion a crossbar to keep it up. Like I said, one must continually be prepared to adapt out here.

As the days got longer, we were able to put in more time pulling the sleds each day, making over eight hours of actual travel time. Our loads were lighter now, weighing approximately 290 pounds since we were losing close to three pounds per day in fuel and food. They were still miserable to pull, but we were able to manage the weight. The extra layer of fat we had accumulated while waiting in Resolute was melting away, and surprisingly, it felt like we were getting stronger. Later, of course, even the muscle would start to fade away, but now we were really starting to hit our stride. Once my knee stopped aching, I was confident that nothing would stop us.

As I reread my blog-post draft, sitting inside the tent on the night of day 14, I was feeling pretty good. My knee was rapidly improving, and I

Overleaf: Ryan works his way through some ice rubble.

was able to walk normally now. Even though I had moments of frustration on the ice with Ryan—he still deferred to me on most decisions—his confidence was improving. Plus, we had just logged our biggest day yet, covering 4.82 miles while navigating through some amazingly huge pressure ridges. As I uploaded my blog, I wondered what Maria and Merritt were doing back home. Hopefully I would dream about them tonight, but only a little. Parading thoughts and images of things that you don't have and might not ever see again is a dangerous game.

Day 14: Brain Freeze

I always forget there are two sides to my polar adage: where there's good ice, bad ice will surely follow. You see (of course you do because it's not that complicated) it works both ways.

Last night we were camped along one of, actually scratch that, THE biggest section of pressured ice I've ever seen: huge blue blocks heaved and fractured together. There was absolutely no way through. But . . .

There was a way around. We headed west until we found a low notch and managed to wiggle our sleds through with only a few big heaves.

"Better than a stick in the eye," I told Ryan afterwards.

For some reason, I've been using that phrase a lot lately . . . along with, "it could be worse." After all, it could be worse. I'm not exactly sure how, but it could be.

Actually, I've learned to moderate my optimism as well as my pessimism. Normally, I'm a "glass is more than half full" guy, but here I work diligently to meter my expectations. As physically difficult as this expedition is, mentally it's even more challenging. The emotional roller coaster of polar travel—I'm sure psychoanalysts out there are just licking their chops hearing about it.

Don't worry about digging deeper though, my head is filled with snow . . . and ice.

The terrain flattened out considerably and we were able to sight on ice several hundred meters away at a stretch. The snow is still drifted and soft enough so we are doing double hauls. Ugh.

The snowshoe back for our second sled was both agonizing and breathtaking. A cold wind stung our faces in the millimeter or two of exposed skin. As much as I just tried to nestle my face deeper in my parka ruff, I couldn't help but steal glances at the blowing snow backlit by the low sun. In the distance further south, the mountains of Ellesmere Island stretched surprisingly far to the east and west.

Right before our soup break, we crossed a lone set of polar bear tracks, made only a few hours prior judging from the amount of drifting, heading to the southwest, and luckily for us, upwind.

Distance traveled: 4.82 nautical miles

Four hours later, I woke up violently shivering inside my sleeping bag. My teeth were literally chattering. At first I thought I must have been dreaming, and lay there thinking it would go away, but it did not. The first thing I notice when I start to move my hands around inside the vapor barrier is that my clothes are damp. I was confused for a moment, until reality hit me: my pee bottle had leaked all over inside my bag, and I was lying in a pool of my own urine. I was so tired last night that I had fallen asleep without sealing it, and it had leaked all over me. I knew right away that this was a potentially dangerous situation. If my sleeping bag gets wet, I am in real trouble, plus once your core drops in temperature, it requires valuable energy reserves to bring it back up. Luckily my clothes soaked up the spill and the bag was safe, but I spent the next hour changing clothes, airing moisture out of the vapor barrier, and then trying to fall back asleep. When dawn arrived much too soon, I cursed myself for my stupidity and a lost hour of valuable sleep. It highlighted the fact that one small mistake can doom the trip. I needed to be more vigilant. Pulling on my urine-soaked clothing that morning before we headed out was miserable. I had dried it

> Once your core drops in temperature, it requires valuable energy reserves to bring it back up.

as best I could, but now I would have to wear it so that it would dry out on the ice the rest of the day. When I told Ryan what had happened, he stifled back a laugh and said, "That sucks, man." What more could he say?

Toward the end of the day, we finally come upon our first real lead. The ice sheets had spread apart the length of at least a football field, exposing the open ocean. The new ice between the sheets is the lead. Newly frozen leads can be one of the most dangerous parts of the trip. If you try to cross them too early and fall through, you can die. By the time we arrived, the lead had probably been refreezing for one day. I skied up to the edge of it and firmly slammed my pole into the ice. Generally if you can hit ice three to four times with your pole and it doesn't go through, it is safe enough to ski out on. After the second hit, my pole started to break through. At only 1.5 inches thick, the ice was not safe enough to go out on. I knew that this crossing was going to be a tough one. Ryan had not yet skied on a lead this size or this fresh, and the ice bending under your skis can make even the toughest minds crack.

At only 1.5 inches thick, the ice was not safe enough to go out on.

Crossing your first big lead is a right of passage for polar explorers. Salt water, unlike freshwater, is very elastic when it first starts to freeze. The newly forming sheet of ice will literally flex under your skis. It's like skiing on rubber. As you move across it, you can feel the ice bowing underneath you, and you can even see a ripple out in front of your skis under the ice. It's disconcerting, to say the least, because you feel like the ice is going to break underneath you. In reality, it's usually strong enough to support your weight—for the most part. Unlike freshwater, if a crack does form, it degrades the entire area, and the whole sheet disintegrates around you, making it very, very hard to get yourself out of the water. The first time I crossed it, I was terrified, so I knew Ryan had to be nervous. "Let's camp here tonight and, hopefully, by the morning it will have frozen over enough to cross," I said. He quickly agreed. Tomorrow morning, if luck was on our side, we would save nearly two hours by crossing the lead directly versus skiing around.

Chapter 5

Walking in Their Footsteps

Coordinates: 83.34 degrees north, 399 miles to North Pole

On July 6, 1908, the SS *Roosevelt* set sail from New York City. On board was 52-year-old Robert Peary and a team of 19 hand-picked men he would be leading on his seventh trip to the Arctic. Since his first expedition to the region in 1886, he had become obsessed with the desire to be the first person to reach the North Pole. He had achieved many accolades in his career, but the pole still eluded him. In fact, he had lost eight toes to frostbite from earlier visits. On board the ship, which was designed specifically for their voyage, were 49 Inuit men, women, and children, 246 sled dogs, 70 tons of whale meat, 50 walrus carcasses, over a dozen sleds, hunting gear, and 330 tons of coal. They anchored off of Cape Sheridan on eastern Ellesmere Island with Greenland in sight. This small army built their own city on shore as winter settled upon them. Igloos dotted the landscape, the hunters kept them fed, and preparations were made for the fast-approaching start date for Peary's latest attempt on the pole.

Like many of history's famous attempts to be first, Peary was employing a siege mentality for this expedition. He would use rotating teams of sleds to continually ferry supplies deeper and deeper into the ice. As he moved north, the caches would supply the team. Instead of tents, they would build igloos each night and would stay warm with coal fires. Their clothing was the same that the Inuit wore, made from caribou hides, sealskin, and fox and wolf fur. After his many years in the north, Peary had learned from the Eskimos and adopted many of their methods.

Overleaf: Ryan crosses his first big lead.

On February 28, 1909, the expedition kicked off as the first teams went out on the ice. Even though they encountered several large leads that stymied their progress—the largest was a quarter-mile wide and stalled them for seven days—by April 1, he was only 133 miles from his goal. He had already made it farther north than any other human in history. Peary, with his assistant Matthew Henson, the four best Inuit sled drivers, five sleds, and 40 dogs, departed for the pole. For the next five days, they averaged over 20 miles per day, and claimed to reach the pole on April 6. He took out his sextant (used by every explorer until GPS; they are notoriously finicky and very hard to use) and made the appropriate readings. After overnighting, they began the perilous over-ice return, following their tracks and sleeping in the igloos they had built during the first leg. When they reached base camp April 23, they were understandably exhausted. They were the first to have gone into the great unknown and returned successfully. Almost immediately Peary was embroiled in a battle with Frederick A. Cook, who claimed to have reached the pole almost a year earlier but had been delayed returning to civilization for almost a year. The controversy dominated the headlines for a year, until Cook's claim was discredited. In the decades since, Peary's own claim has been called into question, with many experts believing he was 30 to 60 miles short of his ultimate goal. Regardless, his voyage of almost two months on the ice was in itself a significant accomplishment, especially in 1908.

I think I can understand how Peary must have felt on his trip. At 52, he knew it would be his final chance to claim one of the last great prizes from the age of exploration. Only three years earlier, he had made it to 87.6 degrees north before being turned back. In 2005, when Lonnie and I had been thwarted after a few weeks on the ice, I was crestfallen. Peary's disappointment must have been of an order of magnitude higher than mine. He had spent a good part of his adult life exploring the wild parts of our planet, and his drive to reach the pole pushed him to extremes.

> In 2005, when Lonnie and I had been thwarted after a few weeks on the ice, I was crestfallen.

Even though we had only been on the ice for 15 days, I also found myself fixated on reaching our goal. Yes, I had been there twice before, but there was a good chance that this also would be my last opportunity to achieve something special with a trip to the North Pole. Only 47 people had ever done what we were attempting—traveling unsupported and unaided from land to the pole. More importantly, I was shooting footage every day for the documentary that Animal Planet was financing. I was excited to share this story with the world, but it would only work if we got there. Ryan had his own lofty goal of being the first American to complete the Explorers Grand Slam—reach the top of the Seven Summits and both poles. As we struggled to gain any forward momentum, these goals weighed heavily on our minds, pushing us to take increasingly danger-ous risks. One of the first rules of staying alive in extreme situations is to know when to step back. I worried that the line was becoming blurred as the days slipped away.

● ● ●

The next morning, day 16, dawned clear and cold, with temperatures hov-ering around minus 30 degrees. We packed up quickly, and stood on the edge of the lead. The crisp night had thickened the ice a couple of inches, and the hoarfrost crystals covering it were much larger as well (always a good sign). I was impatient to get going and felt that we could save a huge amount of time by

With every step we took, my frustrations stepped up a notch.

going directly across the lead versus around it. Looking to the east and west, the thin ice seemed to stretch on forever. Going around just didn't seem like a viable option. Ryan was nervous so we started to head east looking for thicker ice. We felt like we covered a good distance the day prior, but the final tally was only three miles. We knew we needed to be making better mileage. The pressure was palpable.

With every step we took, my frustrations stepped up a notch. I knew where we needed to go. We needed to go out on the ice. I thought: This scouting is a waste of time, and at a certain point, you've got to take the risk and commit. You've got to be willing to just do it. We had covered only 30 miles in two weeks. We couldn't afford any delays. We must keep heading north. And there's a good amount of frost on the ice.

I turned to Ryan and said, "This is it, and there's no reason to keep looking. You are just going to have to get used to the fact that the ice is going to be a little less stable than you like." I turned toward the ice and skied out onto it without waiting to hear his reply. Sometimes you just have to stop screwing around and act.

The first stretch of ice was relatively stable—bending slightly, but still strong enough to support our weight. For a few minutes, we marveled at the unobstructed expanses, and the ease at which we were able to pull our sleds. After 300 yards, the ice turned from gray to black—a telltale indicator of thin ice. In a few spots we could see a seam of open water where the ice hadn't frozen solid yet. We moved to the east, looking for a better path. Ryan was understandably nervous. It is more than a little disconcerting to ski onto very thin ice that bends under foot.

While the ice may have been somewhat borderline as I went across, I just concentrated on keeping my skis wide apart and my arms out wide to spread my weight evenly over the ice. The trick is to be as smooth as possible and never stop. In a few minutes I made it to a small island of multiyear ice that had frozen fast in the middle of the lead. I relaxed as I pulled my sled up onto the more stable sheet and turned back to see how Ryan was doing. He was halfway across, only a few minutes behind me, and his form looked great. I turned forward to see what was awaiting us next. It was another smaller lead, about 50 yards wide, and unfortunately it looked less stable than the one we had just crossed. I could see some surface water on parts of it. We were basically standing on an island of ice surrounded by fresh leads. In the distance, I could see solid ice. But there was no way I would turn around and go back. I would find a way across.

There was only one option: keep moving forward and get to the other side as fast as possible.

I could hear Ryan approaching as I skied with my sled out a few feet on the second lead. Right away I knew I had made a mistake. I could feel the rubber ice flex under my feet, and I could also feel the tails of my skis slowly start to sink through the ice. I tried to turn around to get out of this frozen quicksand, but each movement caused me to sink a bit farther. There was only one option: keep moving forward and get to the other side as fast as possible. I started to ski farther out onto the ice, dragging my sled behind me. The next two minutes were some of the most terrifying of my life. All I could do was focus on the other side. I could feel my ski tails breaking through with every step. One moment of hesitation and I would go through. Ryan told me later it was one of the scariest things he had ever seen. Every time I went forward, my skis were emerging from the ocean water, and my sled was floating. All of the ice was gone behind me. When I got to the other side, I was violently shaking all over, and I could feel the adrenaline coursing through my body. I fumbled to pull my camera out from under my jacket to film myself. Just behind me, the sled was still floating on the water. It was the most dangerous thing I had ever done in my life.

After a few minutes, I was able to relax a bit and I started to look across for Ryan. He had headed farther east on the island, looking for a better place to cross. As I struggled to pull my sled out of the water, I kept looking at him skiing farther away. By skiing east, we would lose any advantage we had gained skiing across the lead in the first place. The tower of tensions from the past two weeks came tumbling down, fueled by a healthy dose of adrenaline from the fear I had just experienced. I could not believe he was not crossing. I unclipped from my sled and started to yell across to

Within a few seconds, his skis started to break through the ice as I watched him struggle to keep moving forward.

him. "C'mon, goddammit. Get on the ice. Quit fucking around. We need to get moving. What are you doing? Just cross." When he yelled back at me, saying that he wasn't sure it was safe, I lost it. I must have looked like a madman, hopping around on the ice bellowing at Ryan. "Just cross here dammit," I screamed at him. "Go, go, go."

Ryan approaches some large blocks of ice.

Ryan turned toward me, shrugged, and went out on the ice. It was about 30 yards across. Within a few seconds, his skis started to break through the ice as I watched him struggle to keep moving forward. He was no more than five feet onto the ice and he was slowly sinking into the water. I felt helpless as I watched him struggle to pull himself forward and out of the water. He grabbed his poles above the baskets and used the picks to pull himself forward as his feet disappeared from sight. Luckily, he made it to a small island of ice and was able to pull himself out before he sank any lower. He quickly crossed to the other side of the island and went back out on more thin ice. He was no more than half the way across the remaining gap when the ice started to disintegrate under him again. This time he sank in up to his waist as he struggled to pull himself out of the dangerously cold water. Using his poles, he was able to slowly crawl toward the edge of the thicker ice, where he slowly extracted himself from the ocean water. The whole crossing had taken no longer than a few minutes, but as I watched, it seemed like hours. All I could do was shout directions to him. I did not even have my rope on me. It was in my sled, several hundred feet away, where I had abandoned it to yell at Ryan.

The moment he made it onto the ice shelf with me, I took control. I knew that if we did not act quickly there was an excellent chance of hypothermia setting in. In minus 30 degrees, a wet body can drop to a dangerously low temperature within minutes. I fell to my knees and popped his skis off; thank God they had not fallen off in the water. As I pulled his sled out of the water, I told him to roll around in the snow—as mentioned earlier, the snow was so dry that it could actually pull the seawater out of his clothes. I tore open his

> While he changed, I apologized repeatedly. It was my fault he had fallen through.

sled to get out his dry clothes—man, was his sled a mess. I found his down jacket and tossed it to him. "Run around while I find your clothes, keep your heart beating fast," I told him. Even though he was acting very calm and cool, you never know when shock can set in. Ryan needed my help.

"Are you cold? Do you feel OK?" I kept asking him while he changed out of his wet gear. He was soaked up to the bottom of his chest, and his clothes were freezing solid as he took them off. While he changed, I apologized repeatedly. It was my fault he had fallen through. I lost control of my emotions and had badgered him into making a potentially life-threatening decision. The fact that he was 30 pounds heavier than me and therefore would have more issues on the thin ice had never crossed my mind. As I pulled the sopping-wet liners out of his boots, he looked at me and said, "Holy crap, that was kind of terrifying. Let's not do that again." I smiled and apologized for the hundredth time while I used an old trick that Borge Ousland, a legendary Norwegian polar explorer, had taught me, and put heavy-duty plastic bags into his boots before inserting his dry backup liners. The shells would be wet but his feet would stay dry.

Overleaf: Eric and Ryan move through a huge pressure ridge.

Sheer force was often needed to move the sleds.

"What were you thinking as you went through?" I asked.

"Not much. I just focused on using my poles to get me out and kept crawling forward. My main fear was losing my skis. Let's get geared up and head out. No reason to stay here any longer." I agreed; we had wasted an hour on this ordeal, and it was time to head north again. By nightfall we were another 2.93 miles closer to our goal, Ryan was a little chillier, and I was still feeling guilty. But those minutes of terror had brought us back to working together as a team. Had the day been windier and colder, Ryan could have easily died. It was another small stroke of luck.

One week later, we were almost 40 miles farther north and had finally broken free of the incessant shattered landscape that had dogged us for so long. The week had quickly gone by in a blur of long days pulling the sleds followed by evenings inside the tent recuperating and refueling. For the first few days after Ryan fell through the ice, we continued to struggle to gain any momentum. On day 17 we gained 3.1 miles, and on

Skiing on a fresh lead

day 18 we hit 3.72. The turning point came on the morning of day 19. It was a clear, beautiful day and the two of us decided that we were done ferrying loads forward. The hours and miles wasted each time we headed backward to bring up the next load were killing us. We would never get close to the pole at this pace. We both were in agreement that, moving forward, we would pull our own sleds. That first day was hard— really hard—but when we checked in that night, we were rewarded with 7.74 miles. Through snowstorms, bitter cold, bruised bodies, and taxing soft snow, we started ticking off miles for the next three days—7.94, 8.83, and 7.90. I was still struggling with missing my family. Many nights I found myself crying silently in my sleeping bag as I read e-mails from Maria telling me about the adventures she and Merritt had that day, but overall I was falling into a pattern. I had been gone for over a month; the time and distance were helping.

Looking back after crossing a large lead

On day 23, the temperature finally warmed up enough, to a manageable minus 20, that it was possible to listen to music while skiing. I got to do something I had been dreaming of for the past week. After a quick route check with my compass, I reached inside my pants pocket where I keep my Nokia and pressed play. As I heard the first guitar notes to "Good Arms versus Bad Arms" by Frightened Rabbit ring out, I smiled. A symphony of sound filled my ears, and the first few lines transported me instantly away from this pain and suffering. Looking out of my goggles, I felt like I was inside of a movie: the goggles frame the landscape, and the music has enveloped me. It's magical. I could not be any happier at this moment. I can finally listen to some tunes while laboring over the ice, and I have a relatively clear path in front of me. I cannot tell you what a huge lift this is to the soul. As I lean into my harness, I am struck by how much this reminds me of skiing to the South Pole.

When I first made it to Antarctica in 2008, it was a crucial moment in my life. I had just recently completed my first successful trip to the North Pole with Lonnie, and I was starting to question my life's direction. It was a difficult time. I was dealing with a couple of failed relationships. I seriously questioned my ability to keep moving forward. On more than one occasion, I thought realistically about giving it all up, pulling the plug, and getting a real job. But Antarctica changed all that.

The small community of polar adventurers I encountered in Antarctica were amazing. For the first time in my life, I felt like people actually understood me. Over the course of the trip I guided to the pole, I came to realize that this was the lifestyle I wanted, and it reignited a passion that is still burning brightly today.

While many people think of both the South and North Poles as similar, the reality is that they are complete opposites. Yes, they're both cold—in fact, Antarctica is, on average, 15 degrees colder than the Arctic—and each one has five months of daylight followed by five months of darkness, but that is where the comparisons stop. Antarctica is a continent, with over 98 percent of the land permanently immersed in ice. It's estimated that the sheets of ice covering the continent hold 90 percent of all the ice on the planet. Best estimates are that in some spots, the ice is close to 2.5 miles thick, meaning that at some locations—the South Pole, for example—the elevation is over 9,000 feet. The ice on the Arctic Ocean, by comparison, reaches a maximum thickness of roughly six or seven feet. Antarctica is covered by an ice cap and slow-moving glaciers, so when skiing to the South Pole, you very rarely have to detour off course. Even though Antarctica is remote, resupply drops are easy to arrange, as the logistics—and, more importantly, what's required to land a plane—are fairly straightforward. None of this is to say that it's easy to get to the South Pole. It is a hard trip. It's just that getting to the North Pole is exponentially more difficult.

Overleaf: Looking down into a crack in the ice

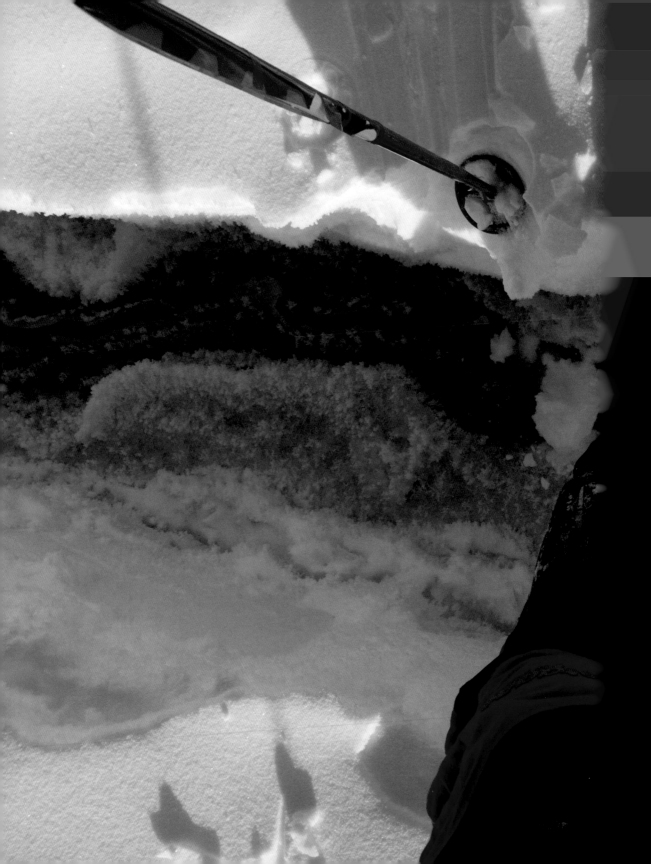

• • •

In 1911, when the two competing teams of legendary polar explorers Robert Falcon Scott and Roald Amundsen both set off for the interior of Antarctica, not much was known about the continent. Given its vast size—it's equal to the United States and Mexico combined—and the minefields of icebergs and vast sheets of pack ice guarding it, very few had penetrated the interior. The size and scope of their endeavors were mind-boggling. Both teams arrived over six months before they were to depart for the pole, spending months hauling supplies progressively deeper into the continent to build up caches for their expedition to the pole and, more importantly, their return. Scott landed with 65 men, 19 ponies, and three motorized sleds to aid in his attempt.

> The size and scope of their endeavors were mind-boggling.

Amundsen had 19 men and more than 100 sled dogs. Each team had several tons of supplies that they needed to survive the polar winter before they could set out the following spring. The difference between the two plans was evident from the start. Amundsen was going to use skis and dogsleds, something his Norwegian team was quite adept at. Scott's British team had an aversion to dogs and skis and, instead, was relying on ponies to haul gear. They had a few dogs but were planning on pulling their own sleds.

The two groups departed only 13 days apart, but already Amundsen had an advantage over his rival. From his starting point on the Bay of Whales, he was already 60 miles closer to his goal than Scott, something he had planned in advance. For the next 60 days, he and his team of five worked their way progressively south with four sleds and 52 dogs. Part of the way to the pole, they slaughtered all but 18 of the dogs for food and rations for their way back. Dressed in Inuit-style furs and skins, they were warm and comfortable. When they reached the South Pole on December 17, 1911, they had been on the continent for almost an entire year and gone from home over 18 months. They spent one day at the pole before leaving a note for Scott, a tent, and the Norwegian flag flying. All of Amundsen's team plus 11 dogs returned to their starting point, 39 days later. It was one of the most celebrated feats of its time. Amundsen's use of skis and sleds and the adoption of Inuit equipment and clothing (much like Robert Peary) were hailed as groundbreaking, and laid out a road map for a generation of explorers to come. After returning, Amundsen embarked on several other expeditions and, in 1926, became

Scott's expedition was doomed from the beginning.

the first person to fly to the North Pole. He disappeared in June 1928 while flying a rescue mission in the Arctic.

Scott's expedition was doomed from the beginning. Unlike the Norwegians, he and his team were laboring in woolen clothes that while keeping them warm when active, were insufficient for the subzero temperatures and would later contribute to numerous cases of frostbite. Within days of starting out, the motor sleds failed. They had already lost almost half of the ponies they had brought with them due to various injuries and accidents, and those remaining began to die. There had been plans to equip the ponies with snowshoes, which might have helped, but it was never tried. Forty days in, as they were starting to climb up toward the Antarctic Plateau, over 5,000 feet above them, Scott sent back the dogs, shot the ponies, and the remaining team of 12 men continued on foot, pulling their supplies. Eleven days later, Scott sent four men back to the coast as the remaining eight continued forward, half on skis and half on foot. Eleven days later, when three more men were sent back and the remaining five continued forward, they were still close to 200 miles away. They finally reached the pole on January 17, 1912, a full month behind Amundsen. The disappointment must have been crushing. The return trek out turned into a death march, as the five men slowly started to fall apart from malnutrition and exhaustion. On March 29, 1912, Robert Falcon Scott recorded his last diary entry:

> We had fuel to make two cups of tea apiece and bare food
> for two days on the 20th. Every day we have been ready to
> start for our depot 11 miles away, but outside the door of the

tent it remains a scene of whirling drift. I do not think we can hope for any better things now. We shall stick it out to the end, but we are getting weaker, of course, and the end cannot be far.

It seems a pity, but I do not think I can write more.

R. SCOTT.

For God's sake look after our people.

At this point, only three of them were still alive, and they had been on the ice for an astounding 149 days. When their bodies were found eight months later, all three of them were tucked inside their sleeping bags. Both teams had faced the great unknown and accomplished something incredible. But Scott illustrates the brutal consequences of a cascading series of miscalculations.

• • •

As I lay in my tent on the night of day 23, looking at my GPS unit to calculate how far we had come, I thought about Scott on the ice, suffering while Amundsen celebrated. I wondered what the great explorers would think of the two of us sitting here right now. Much like them, we were dealing with unknown conditions as we struggled to make our way forward, driven by the need to reach an arbitrary point on a map. Ryan and I were both driven by very specific goals, and were increasingly finding ourselves getting closer to exceeding the edge of "safe" decision-making. The conditions we were facing were much different than explorers had faced a century ago. The ice was so much thicker and more stable back when Peary and his team ventured

> I thought about Scott on the ice, suffering while Amundsen celebrated.

Left: Ryan crosses a large crack in a pressure ridge.

Overleaf: Navigating through less than ideal ice

out to the pole. They had to overcome bigger pressure ridges, but once they broke free of the shore ice, they were able to travel for whole days on massive pans of ice. Using dogsleds, they made the pole in an astounding 37 days, still one of the fastest times ever.

The last successful trip to the North Pole by dogsled was in 2005, due to the rapidly changing nature of the ice. That same year, I made my first summer attempt at the pole with Lonnie. The days of traveling for a whole day on one large pan of ice are gone. In its place is many smaller pans that are continually tearing apart and crashing back together, forming numerous leads and pressure ridges. It is too dangerous to take dogs out anymore. I can only imagine what Peary or Scott would think of our modern communications equipment. Of course, I wonder what Peary or Scott would think of the fact that I am able to type and publish expedition updates in the middle of the polar ice sheet. It might not be that foreign to them, since they filled out daily diaries describing their trips. What might be a bit more surprising to them is the GPS unit that pinpoints location, or the DeLorme inReach transmitter that continually sends out location updates. They were using a sextant to calculate their location, and once they left home, they were out of contact with their families for years until they returned. The idea of me looking at pictures of Maria and Merritt in the tent each night would probably make them chuckle. They didn't have time for nonsense like that. They were trying to stay alive in an unknown world. They didn't have the luxury of calling for a plane to rescue them if things went south. They either succeeded or died trying.

Typing the blog update later that night, I realized how lucky I was to be out here attempting this endeavor. So many times during the day, I would find myself questioning my decision to come back to this dangerous place. When you spend the day on an endless conveyer belt of crap and pain, it's easy to get downhearted. But with a little luck, a lot of heart, and some good tunes, I felt able to keep moving forward. I am driven to

> The idea of me looking at pictures of Maria and Merritt in the tent each night would probably make them chuckle.

get to the pole and tell its story. There are certain times out here when the overwhelming beauty of this place takes your breath away. Even sitting in this stinky tent across from Ryan, it was magical to be here.

Day 23: The Polar Grind

Another day on the ice and we were left with more than ample time to contemplate nearly every imaginable topic. Well, at least general topics. To think about our lives, as they may exist when we are finished is a dangerous thing.

It's warmed up enough (you know to minus 20) that I've finally got my Nokia Windows phone playing music for part of the day while I'm skiing and it's definitely a welcome distraction—although many of the songs remind me of previous expeditions—for better or worse.

We struggled for the entire first hour of the day trying to find any larger pans. The soft snow was still tugging at our sleds and we feared it was going to be another brutal slog of a day (it was but not as bad as yesterday). Next shift, I got lucky and found an older frozen lead to follow for about 400 meters. Then through some really beautiful blue blocks of pressure, some small pans and then something moderately better.

Halfway through my shift Ryan realized he had dropped his outer mitts. He skied back to where we had filmed a short distance back, but no mitts. Luckily he had a spare pair.

I've been haunted by my dreams the past few nights—not that they're particularly bad, it's just that they seem so real. When I wake up I it takes me a while to figure out which is reality and which is dream.

Today at soup break we talked about some of the things we appreciate more because we have so little out here. For me, there is one simple act that never fails to amaze me when I'm home: the moment I get into bed and feel the softness of the mattress. So nice.

Not that I necessarily need a mattress to be comfortable. I've always believed comfort is a state of mind. Here our two ThermaRest pads each are luxury enough, but still . . .

Ryan talked about going to a movie, "I'd wear lots of clothes—so I'm warm—then get a big popcorn, soda and a coffee and just sit and relax."

We ended the day with surface conditions improving slightly and a beautiful sundog / halo to our left. Perfectly arced rainbows framed a low yellow sun and another beam of light appeared directly below the sun extending straight down.

Amazing and beautiful.

Distance traveled: 8.16 nm

Chapter 6

Stretched Too Thin

Coordinates: 84.39 degrees north, 336 miles to North Pole

"Fuck you, Eric. Quit telling me what to do, godammit!" Ryan screamed down at me from atop a 10-foot-tall chunk of ice. "Fuck this stupid movie, fuck the shot you want, and fuck you." Above Ryan, the sky had recently switched from clear skies to an ominous gray that's usually a precursor to a storm, but right now, it made Ryan look like a frozen version of Charlton Heston in *The Ten Commandments*. Instead of holding tablets above his head, he was holding our camera as he yelled down at me. "I will shoot whatever scene I want, dammit," he bellowed at me. "I am sick of this shit." Part of me wanted to laugh out loud, he looked so comical ranting down at me, but at the same time, I completely understood why he was angry—he had every right to be. But I was angry, too. For 23 days, I had been handling a majority of the filming while constantly asking him to help more. I had tried every approach over the past week, and we had had several heart-to-heart talks about a solution. He knew it was important, but daily survival was a higher priority for him. But we had made a commitment to film. After texting Corinna from High Noon, the Colorado production company overseeing our documentary, this morning, we had set one specific goal: both of us would get a shot skiing toward the camera, so our "faces" could be seen. The last thing on our list, and not even on the agenda for the day, was a shot from above, like the one he was filming.

"Fuck you, dude. We just talked about this a few hours ago," I shouted back. "You are shooting the dumbest shot ever." I pushed through the rubble toward the gap in the ice ahead of me. He screamed back, "I can't fucking walk backward through this ice with the camera, asshole," even

Overleaf: Stuck in hell

At times, it took hours to cover just a few hundred feet.

madder now. I hoped he wouldn't fall down. I stopped and looked up at him. "Whatever, man. Don't film. I don't care," I yelled, and then I started to walk forward, dragging my sled behind me. The nice thing about wearing goggles and a nose beak is that no one can see how you really look. I might have looked composed, but under my goggles and face mask I was fuming. Everything about this damn trip had been a pain in the ass so far. This was just par for the course.

Our 24th day had started clear and beautiful with good ice, but halfway through, the ice rubble reappeared with a vengeance and the weather turned terrible. We were traversing a never-ending series of small ice pans, each one bordered by a pressure ridge. Now, 50 feet from Ryan, there was a four-foot lip of ice blocking my path. Without even stopping to look back, I climbed it and powered my sled up to the top, trying to get as much distance between Ryan and myself as possible. I veered back and forth with my head spinning as I struggled to figure out how to navigate the puzzle all around me.

Indecision. Both ways look like a bad idea.

My frustration was mounting. We were almost halfway into our food and fuel supplies, and all we had to show for it was a paltry 95.2 miles of progress. We still had so far to go. To make the pole in the remaining 26 days we had left, we would have to average almost 15 miles a day. Our expedition planning was based on being on the ice for 50 days; our fuel and food were designed to run out after that. Sure, we had five days of emergency rations, but those were really for sustaining us in case we were stuck on the ice waiting for the plane to pick us up from the pole—not nearly enough calories to sustain a full day's skiing effort. The logistics were starting to fray at the seams. The last thing we needed was for our relationship to fall apart. Many an expedition has been undone by harsh words and bad blood.

When I finally got up onto a flat pan again and looked behind me, I could see Ryan was having a hard time getting through the rough ice.

Overleaf: Navigating in poor weather conditions

Part of me wanted to let him keep struggling, but I knew that was the wrong thing to do. I unhooked my sled and started to walk back to him.

For the rest of the day, any momentum that we gained earlier was completely lost.

"Dude, I'm sorry for micromanaging you. I get it why you're mad at me," I said as I approached him. "I thought we had discussed it this morning, and as you know with me, when we say we are going to do something, that's what I do, no exceptions." He stopped pulling his sled and looked up at me. I could see myself reflected in his goggles, framed against the swirling sky. "It's OK man, I'm sorry too," he replied. I went behind him and pulled hard on the back handle of his sled to help him escape the maze.

An hour later, as we sat huddled behind a towering block of ice sipping our lunch soup, I thought about the 87th parallel. We were starting to gain some momentum. It seemed that we had finally broken free of the truly rotten ice that had plagued us at the start. Granted, we were not making the daily mileage we needed to get to the pole. But hopefully the farther north we traveled, the better the ice would get. Instead of looking at the almost insurmountable number of miles left, I decided we should focus on reaching the 87th parallel. From there we would be less than 180 miles from our goal. We needed something good to happen. The 163 miles to the 87th was doable, and once there we could reassess. I decided to talk with Ryan about it that night, once we got in from the ice. But at the moment, both of us were still stewing and sipping our lunch in silence. The last thing I needed to do was start taking control of the conversation.

For the rest of the day, any momentum that we gained earlier was completely lost. We were blocked by bad weather and even worse ice. Even though neither of us said more than 10 words to each other, it seemed like we were cooling down. Still, rather than help one another out, we both opted to wrestle our sleds alone through massive truck-size blocks and pressure ridges. It was the worst ice we had experienced the whole trip, and we spent long, straining minutes locked in battles to shift our sled a few inches. Several times, after gaining some hard-won progress, my sled slipped and fell backward into a deep crack. Despite the intense effort, I was actually a bit happy about the fight. Ryan was not one to show much emotion, and I had been telling him for several days that it's OK to be frustrated. Maybe the fight was his way of releasing steam. I let Ryan handle the blog post that night, and it was pretty evident that we were both still smarting a bit.

Day 24: Connect the Dots!

April 7 and oh what a day it was . . . We have been cruising pretty well as of late despite the slow surface conditions. Today we figured would be much the same and it was for the first half.

The conditions were overcast and cold, but some decent visibility so we found a few big flat (ish) pans of ice and made good progress. But around mid day, right around the time we blew up at each other over a detail then squarely apologized, the ice changed dramatically and we found ourselves playing "polar connect the dots" which is not as fun as it may sound. It is basically trying to piece together small open patches in the general direction you are trying to go, all while avoiding the inevitable ice ridges all around you. We did some tough work and ended up taking our sleds up, over, around, and at one point I could swear under, ridges up to 20 feet high of giant blue ice cubes.

We only managed 4.18 nautical miles today but I can say we fought hard for every bit of it. Better luck tomorrow I am sure . . .

Distance traveled: 4.18 nm

When we woke up the next morning, it was cold—almost minus 40—but sunny. That was a good way to start the day. The two of us apologized again for the fight the previous day, and then I told Ryan that I would no longer bug him about filming. From here on out, there would be no pressure on him. I would continue to focus on getting shots every day, and if he wanted to help, that would be great. It was good to be functioning

Ryan crosses a small pressure ridge.

as a team again. In no time we were out on the ice, straining against our harnesses to gain momentum.

We had not seen any significant winds for several days, and it was starting to wear us out. Nearly every morning we were greeted by a light dusting of snow, and while the accumulation totaled only two or three inches, it was enough to slow our progress to an even slower crawl and sap dwindling energy reserves. If the wind would only pick up a few knots, it would blow off the thin layer of snow accumulation and expose a nice hardpack that would allow our sleds to slide much easier. Right now it felt like we were dragging anchors through the sand. My knee was still hurting as I leaned forward, but the pain had died off to a manageable ache. While my knee was getting better, my heart was getting worse. When I e-mailed Maria the previous night, I poured out my heart to her about my homesickness and missing Merritt. She was supportive, but at the same time she didn't offer me much in the way of compassion. She was home with a toddler, running her business full-time, and dealing with being a single parent. Her life was pretty chaotic, too.

I had to deal with my issues in my own way, and one of the stranger coping mechanisms I developed on this trip was having conversations with my sled. When it got bogged down, tipped over, or was just being a pain, I would find myself talking to it just like I would Merritt. When it fell into a big crack, I turned to it and said, "Now why would you do that, little boy? You're just being a silly boy, that's all." Everyone deals with adversity his or her own way; I talk to my sled.

By the time we made it to the tent that night, we both were exhausted. The seven miles we had crossed were hard fought. In the middle of the day, my right foot had started to hurt so bad that I had to stop and take off my boot. The day prior, I had worn a slightly lighter-weight pair of socks and not laced my boot tight enough, and my foot slid just enough inside to aggravate a blister deep inside the ball of my foot. The pain was unbearable, and I worried I might be done. The thought of our expedition being scrubbed due to a blister seemed ridiculous, almost too much for me to bear. As I stood up, the pain lancing out from my foot was blinding, but I found that by arching my foot and balancing on my toes and heel, I was able to continue on. We were 25 days into our journey and both had to deal with a variety of ailments, but we continued onward.

● ● ●

"My God, it feels like I have spent the past 10 hours pulling a truck tire across a beach," Ryan said in the tent on the night of day 28. I had to agree. The lack of wind was wearing both of us down. For the past three days, we were progressively upping our mileage—8.59, 9.73, 9.54—but we were doing it in snow that grabbed and clawed at our sleds, slowing us. The increased mileage had come at a huge cost. We were spending more time on the ice and sleeping less. The convergence of semi-decent ice

Overleaf: Traveling along the edge of a large crack in the ice, trying to find a way across

Traveling under the midnight sun

and good weather had convinced us to spend more time traveling each day. It was the only way we were going to get to the 87th parallel on any reasonable schedule, because it's virtually impossible to speed up out here. One of the limiting factors was how fast we could physically move. Going a rate of a mile an hour—our painfully slow average speed—the only way to knock out more miles is with longer days. And the days were starting to mirror *Groundhog Day*—nothing seemed to change. Wake up, suffer, go to sleep, repeat tomorrow.

The good news this day was that we crossed the 85th parallel. To celebrate, I open one of my small bags of cheese puffs. They were easily the best cheese puffs I've eaten in my life. It only took us seven days to make it here since crossing the previous parallel. Surprising, considering it took us 21 long and painful days to cross the first one. Sadly, at this rate we won't reach the 87th parallel until day 42, leaving us only eight days to traverse the last three degrees to reach the pole. If we continued at even our recent pace, it just didn't add up to get us to the pole. It was hard to look at these numbers and not throw in the towel. Our goal of reaching the North Pole was starting to become an impossibility, but still we focused on it.

To do that, we tried to not look too far into the future out here or to get too hopeful. We just needed to take it one day at a time. Setting a goal of reaching the 87th parallel provided us with a realistic objective to achieve, but there were so many variables to factor that making a plan for after was impossible. We would reassess our situation once we got there.

The endless effort is starting to show on our bodies. After almost a month on the ice, all of the fat we had packed on while sitting around Resolute Bay has melted off. Where we had some extra padding around our stomachs, now you could almost see our ribs. Spending close to 12 hours a day on the ice dragging a sled behind you is the ultimate weight-loss program—though not one most people would sign up for. At this point we were burning close to 8,000 calories a day, and both of us were constantly hungry. No sooner than I ate breakfast, I start to look forward to my first energy bar on the ice. We were fighting a losing battle on the caloric side. We simply cannot eat until we are full, because there is not enough food. One of the harder decisions we had to make when planning the logistics for the trip was how much food to pack. Extra food means extra weight, and after the battles we fought in the first few weeks, I don't think we could have dealt with even one more pound in the sleds.

> We were each pulling our own sleds now, which was great for the mileage, but the constant effort was exhausting.

Besides the loss of weight, both of us are dealing with a variety of ailments. My knee is still sore, my foot is raw, my back is killing me, plus my legs just ache. Ryan's shin was sore from being bashed by the sled, and his hips were getting sore from a worsening cold injury caused by his pants rubbing all day long in the freezing temperatures, on top of dealing with the aches and pains associated with pulling the sleds. We were each pulling our own sleds now, which was great for the mileage, but the constant effort was exhausting. Just trying to get comfortable in the tent is a

chore. Sitting across from me, Ryan looked like a homeless guy, with his bushy beard and messy hair. I'm sure we were also quite ripe due to the sweat—and in my case urine—infusing our outfits.

As I dozed off to sleep, my mind was wrapped around all of the obstacles that had been thrown in our path. We had overcome each one, but I wasn't sure how many more we could beat. Sooner or later, something was going to prove too big. It was almost like the polar gods were laughing at us as they tried to see how much crap we could deal with. The stress of failure was starting to weigh heavily on me, causing my moods to swing about like a kite in a thunderstorm. We needed a break—something had to go our way for once, or we might as well call in the plane and go home.

Two days later, the gods answered our prayers with a vengeance. We awoke on the morning of day 30 to the tent wildly flapping in 45-mile-per-hour wind gusts. The temperature hovered around minus 40, and my breath escaped the sleeping bag in huge clouds of grayish fog. My first thought was that it's going to be a rough day out there, getting blown around in a whiteout. But then I realize that finally we will be free of the powdery snow that is slowing us down. Outside our tent, the ice is a riot of noise. We are surrounded by cracked and moving ice, and you can hear it creaking and squeaking, like Styrofoam blocks rubbing up against each other, plus sound like the chug of a train: *chug, chug, chug*. All of these huge pans seem to be ramming into each other, just feet away from our heads.

The next surprise of the morning is when I crank up the GPS unit and find that we have drifted over five miles to the northeast during the night. The fact that we have moved that much closer to the pole was heartening, but I know not to celebrate this too much. What the Arctic gives, it can rapidly take away. Because the ice sheet has shrunk so much over the past few decades, it now moves around much more than it used to. As the overall extent of sea ice decreases, there is less land-fast ice

Left: Carefully crossing a fresh lead

A large pressure ridge far out on the ice

securely moored to Russia, Canada, Greenland, and Alaska. The prevailing currents control most of the movement, pushing the ice in a southward direction, toward the Canadian coast (which is why the ice is usually the worst there). As the ice cap shrinks and thins, winds have a much more dramatic effect on the movement of pack ice. It's erratic, like a two-year-old on caffeine, and can drive you just as crazy if you think too much about it. We knew that the general drift would be against us, like walking on a treadmill, but we were always hopeful for positive gains as well. More worrisome was drifting east, which could push us way off course as well. More problematic was the time we spent in the tent. During the day, we could counter the negative drift. But while sleeping, miles of hard-won progress were erased in the blink of an eye. Every morning, I marked our position on the GPS and noted how much we drifted. It's something that can break your will if you think too much about it.

The previous day, while we were crossing a large pan, we came across the most amazing thing: we crossed the tracks of Yasu Ogita, the Japanese solo traveler we had met in Resolute. I had almost forgotten that he was out here. I felt like Robinson Crusoe finding a footprint in the sand. It was something you don't expect to find out here. It was both exciting and disappointing that we were not the only people on this wasteland. Looking at his ski tracks, we could tell he was struggling through the same bad snow and a heavy load. I remember wondering back in Resolute Bay how his skis would do out here, since they were much shorter than ours. From looking at his tracks, it seemed he was having issues, floundering around. His tracks were herringboned—where ski tips turn out 45 degrees from the body to ascend for better traction—up short rises where we were able to keep our skis straight. Having to continually switch skiing styles is a huge drain on your energy and something to avoid. We could tell he had been through a few days earlier by the snow that was covering part of his tracks, and the ice

> Now, out on the ice, the blowing snow and wind were mythic.

obviously had moved, since his tracks went off toward the east, not north. I could only hope he was doing OK as we skied away from his path.

After heading out, my hopes for clearer ice were quickly confirmed. The soft, mucky snow was gone, and pulling the sled is measurably better. That was the only positive, though. The whiteout was accompanied by flat light, making it almost impossible to distinguish shapes and distances. Now, out on the ice, the blowing snow and wind were mythic. We were forced to navigate by looking at the direction the wind was blowing the snow across our skis and by taking continual compass bearings to make sure we weren't going in circles. The first hour was pure hell, as we blindly stumbled through a large pressure ridge, trying not to break anything every time we misjudge a step and fall down. Somehow we broke free of the jumbled ice and spent the rest of the day on relatively large, flat pans of ice that we were able to ski steadily across. For the first time of the entire trip, we avoided any real pressure ridges, and I was amazed at our

Overleaf: The ideal lead, frozen over enough to make it easy to cross

Ryan pulls his sled up a rise.

luck, considering we couldn't see. Realistically, I must have simply veered around drifts without even knowing it. Lunch was a frozen affair, and each break was brief in the subzero weather. After 12 hours on the ice we set up camp. It was a physically demanding day, but we covered 11.4 miles. To celebrate, we broke out one of our cans of Pringles and were actually able to smile for a little bit.

Sitting in the tent the next night—day 31—I do some simple math. It took us 12 hours to travel another 11.5 miles, which is great. But if I were back home, I could have driven from Boulder to Minneapolis, 900 miles away, in the same amount of time, or flown across the country . . . twice! It's an interesting commentary on our "normal" lives. At home there is no way I would do solely one thing for 12 hours straight. But here, day after day, that is what I do. Sometimes you don't realize how momentously hard something is until you are in the middle of it.

The drift and wind were on our side again today, and before we even leave the tent we awake slightly closer to our goal. By midday the storm had blown itself out and blue skies had returned. A little over halfway through the day, crossing a large pan, we came across two different sets of polar bear tracks and a set of arctic fox tracks headed toward the northeast. Much like stumbling across Yasu's tracks the other day, these tracks reminded me that we are not the only creatures out here roaming across the ice. But unlike Yasu, these were the tracks of something that would easily kill us. The fox's tracks made me particularly nervous. Up here, arctic foxes are the perennial hangers-on of polar bears.

I made sure the gun was loaded and ready to go in the sled.

They follow them, hoping to eat some of their latest kill. I hoped that would not be us. For the rest of the day, both of us are more observant than ever, and I made sure the gun was loaded and ready to go in the sled.

After a few days of double-digit miles and shorter nights of sleep, I was struggling to type my blog update. I kept dozing off while composing it, until finally I cut it short and sent out a very brief entry. If we could keep up this pace, I foresaw a time soon when I wouldn't be able to devote an hour of my time each night to writing an update. The people following us back home would have to rely on our voicemail posts. If we could keep knocking out the miles, I would have to abandon blogging for the first time ever on an expedition.

Day 31: Polar Potpourri

It was a little mix of everything today. We started in the same whiteout and blowing snow as yesterday. Then we hit some bad pressure ridges, which transitioned into a series of cracks in the ice one of which was actively getting larger.

We saw two sets of polar bear tracks (or the same one going in opposite directions) and arctic fox tracks as well.

We spent also few minutes watching and listening to two sheets of ice grind into each other making a chug, chug sound.

Overall, a pretty eventful day on the ice.

Distance traveled: 11.5 nautical miles

• • •

Four days later, we were 40.3 miles farther north and we were screwed. It was day 35, and we had just crossed the 86th parallel. Just like the last one, it took us seven days to get here. We are maintaining momentum, but at what cost? Every morning it is a struggle to get myself moving. Lethargy and exhaustion are the overwhelming forces at work as I stumble out of the tent. Usually after two to three hours of skiing, I find myself waking up and starting to feel "normal." But it is coming at a heavy price. Each day I find myself getting into my food reserves earlier than planned to find a bit more energy. Hopefully this unplanned snacking won't come back to haunt me later. Whereas earlier in the trip I could stay on Ryan's heels, I now find myself looking at his rapidly disappearing figure in front of me as I flounder forward. Luckily he is comfortable enough by now to take the lead each morning and keep us heading in the right direction. As I slog behind him, my mind more often than not goes to dark places, where I find myself continually questioning my decisions. By now we have entered into the Midnight Sun phase of the Arctic season, where the sun is up 24 hours a day. It won't set again until mid-August. We already are starting to wear down. Less sleep is the last thing we need right now, but it is a reality that both of us are prepared to accept to achieve our goal.

The real problem is that I seriously don't think we can make it to the pole. We have 15 days left to make it, maybe 17 if Elizabeth, our base-camp manager, is able to convince Kenn Borek to give us two more days. But the ice is rapidly deteriorating underneath us. Just the other day, we had to quickly work our way through two sections of ice that were actively pressing into each other. The loud grinding noise sounded like someone was running a wood chipper, and everywhere around us there was movement. I actually watched the ice split between Ryan and his sled as he was navigating a particularly rough section—within 30 seconds, the ice moved him almost three feet from his sled. I have never seen ice moving that fast up here. A little while later, we came upon a lead that stretched as far as the eye could see. It was a young one, with almost definitely bad ice in the middle. We were going to have to cross it, and we would probably get wet. Time to break out our drysuits.

It's hard to fully fathom what swimming in our drysuits is like. First of all, the suits themselves are basically a sack with arms and legs, and a drawstring at the top that cinches up around our heads and faces, so that only our goggles and nose are exposed to the elements. They are made of coated nylon, which means that they are technically not waterproof. The seams are a weak point where the needle poked holes in the water-proofing. (The drysuits are seamed taped, but the material is just coated nylon. It degrades rapidly with use.) Since our drysuits had already been used on a previous expedition, they were somewhat worn and cumbersome to use.

One of the best features of our drysuits was also the worst: to use them, we simply wore them over all of our boots and clothing. That meant we didn't have to adjust layers in the freezing cold. But it also meant that getting inside required carefully working semifrozen drysuit material over big ski boots and the rest of our apparel. I pointed my toes down and slowly slid my boots inside, carefully making sure I didn't tear any part of the fabric. As my toes touched the bottom, I pulled the fabric up around my waist, and then slowly slid my arms inside. With my hands swaddled in material, I fumbled to pull the rest of the suit up and over my head, before one clumsy pull of the drawstring sealed my head. All that was showing was my face.

The whole process of donning the drysuit took 15 minutes, and by the time we were ready to go out on the lead I was frozen.

I went first, towing my sled. The lead itself was not very wide, maybe 100 feet, but the ice looked thin and rotten. I hoped I wouldn't break through. I crawled methodically forward, keeping my weight evenly distributed, trying to choose the best path. But little more than 50 feet in, I started to hear the ice cracking underneath. "I'm going to break through," I yelled back to Ryan. I scampered five more feet forward when I started to feel my knees breaking through—it's a sickening feeling—then my waist was in, and lastly my upper body. Luckily the insulation of the suit and my clothing keeps the cold away.

The clothing and air inside the suit made it very buoyant—so much, in fact, that it was difficult to keep my feet below the water's surface.

Ryan in his survival suit, using his polar picks to crawl across bad ice

Instead of fighting it, I immediately started swimming in a modified back-stroke style, paddling at the air with pinwheeling arms and kicking my feet to push ice chunks out of the way. Turning over, I could see the other side close by, but only for a moment. The suit flipped me back over like a turtle. Through it all, I focused on keeping my head high in the water. If it dipped, water would flow through the face opening and flood the suit with freezing water. One small mistake could mean hypothermia in moments, followed possibly by death. As I reached the other side, relief flowed through my body. Breaking through the ice and swimming had required 100 percent of my focus and energy. I was exhausted, but happy we were across. I looked at Ryan: he had a small smile on his face. He, too, was relieved. This was his first time swimming up here, and I was sure it would not be his last.

The ice is not the biggest of my worries, though. What's really disconcerting is the fact that currently we don't have enough fuel to survive. Even though we had been strictly rationing, the extra moments warming the tents had thrown off our calculations. Up here fuel is life. You can make it with half-rations, broken gear, and injuries. What you can't make it without is fuel, because it is the only way to make water. Without the stoves, we can't melt down the snow each morning and night. By my best estimates, we have 12 days of fuel left at our current rate of consumption. If we could somehow stretch it long enough to make it to the pole, there's still the ever present fear that we could be stranded out here for days, maybe even weeks, if the weather gets bad and the plane can't get to us. That would be a death sentence—a slow and painful one.

That night in the tent, as I am pondering our choices, Ryan received an e-mail about an avalanche in the Khumbu Icefall on Mount Everest between Base Camp and Camp 1. A large group of Sherpas, many of them friends of his, were killed when a large serac collapsed as they were ferrying gear up the mountain. I could see his shoulders sag as he thought about it. The loss of life was staggering. It was another weight thrown on him out here.

As we sat in the tent, we discussed our options and were confronted with a decision that had our lives hanging in the balance. Our dwindling fuel reserves meant that any margin of safety was gone. We could call in the plane now, but that would mean abandoning the trip and letting down everyone who has loaned us money. We had raised almost $200,000 and we would go back with nothing to show for it except broken dreams. We could also continue on to the 87th parallel and reassess then. Plus it would cost us about $10,000 more if we are picked up there instead of here. Not a cheap decision to make. One thing was certain: fuel rationing had to be put in place immediately. No more hot water bottles for the sleeping bags, and no extra warming the tent. The stove can only be used to dry essential gear, melt water, and cook food. Things were about to get even bleaker. The two of us decided to sleep on it and make our decision in the morning.

In the morning, day 36, we decided to head farther north and see if the tide of bad luck would finally turn for us. We were definitely due for some good karma out here. Historically, most expeditions have reported that once past the 87th parallel, the ice tends to get better. It's where the final sprint usually begins. We could only hope that ours would get under way there also.

That day, we each broke through the ice while crossing some sketchy leads. I sunk up to my thighs but managed to leap free, onto a more solid piece of ice, before sinking any farther. My bibs and boots kept my feet mostly dry, and I rubbed snow on myself to dry off and kept skiing to stay warm. It was near the end of the day, and I thought it would be better to just keep moving than to waste time changing into dry clothes. Still, it was cold, windy, and overcast. Stopping for just a minute brought on violent shivers. I didn't want to stop for fear of getting frostbite. Earlier in the day, we had crossed Yasu's track again, and this time they seemed to be heading mostly in our same direction. They only looked a few days old, so we knew we were catching up to him. He still looked to be struggling with his short skis.

Late that afternoon, I crested a small pressure ridge, looked north, and saw Yasu's orange tent ahead of us. "No way," I said out loud to myself. In my mind, there was absolutely no way that we would see Yasu. On the Arctic Ocean, every decision leads to another set of decisions that, in turn, leads to yet another series of navigational decisions. With so many variables and a constantly moving surface, the chances of seeing the only other expedition are a million to one. I was already dumbfounded to have crossed his tracks. And now this. Yasu in his tent. I had also assumed that Yasu was at least two days ahead of us

The closer we got, I could see that there was a fair amount of snow drifted around it, a sign that it had been up for at least two days. We hollered out a greeting and his head poked out of the opening, sheathed in a black stocking cap, his body wrapped in a space blanket. He told us that he had abandoned his bid two days ago, due to his shrinking store of rations and fuel. He was at 86.11 degrees north and 233 miles from the pole. The ice in the beginning had stymied him as much as it had us, and he had left eight days before we had. Kenn Borek's team thought they would be able to get him in three to four more days, when the weather cleared up. For a fleeting moment, I thought about asking him for some of his extra fuel, but decided against it. We would either succeed or fail

Yasu waiting for the plane to pick him up

on our own. By the time we made camp that night, I was fairly frozen and we had knocked another 10.63 miles off our remaining distance. Soon we would be the only ones left out on the ice. While I was sad that Yasu was abandoning his expedition, I couldn't help but be a little envious. He had put in a great effort and now he was relaxing in his tent, burning extra fuel and eating whenever he felt like it. There would be no such earthly pleasures for us. We were truly on our own now.

I hit rock bottom three days later, day 39. We had covered 34.6 miles in three days, but an e-mail from home had broken my spirit. Maria and Merritt had gone to a friend's house for a party, and Merritt had called two other guys Daddy. As I read those words over and over, I began to cry uncontrollably. The fact that my son didn't know who his dad was broke my soul into a thousand pieces. The prevailing thought going over and over in my head was, why continue? Why go on? We are just going to die out here, and my son will never know who I was. I will just be some person that he reads about. I was the selfish father who wanted to risk his

Ryan leading in the middle of a windstorm

life to go back to the dangerous place he had already been twice before. I would be the father who had ignored repeated warning signs to turn back before it was too late.

When I told Ryan what was going on and how I was feeling, he succinctly stated what I already knew. "You have to dial that shit in." His words hit home. Ryan is a guy of few words, but when he speaks, it's best to listen. I knew that he had been struggling for the past few days, with worsening frostbite on his legs and his fair share of low points as well. Just the other day, he had told me during a lunch break that he felt like he was in the midst of a bad country song, titled "Why Am I Always Crying in My Goggles?"

I didn't know if I could go on mentally, physically, or emotionally. I was at the end of my rope. I decided to go to sleep and make a decision in the morning about whether to continue or to pull the plug and head back home to my family.

Chapter 7

Ready, Set, Go

Coordinates: 86.83 degrees north, 190 miles to North Pole

When I woke up the next morning, I felt like a huge pressure has been lifted from my shoulders: my connection to home was disappearing. We had been out on the ice for 40 days now, and the attachments to the "normal" world were starting to fade away.

On every expedition I have been on, after seven weeks I experience what I liked to call the Day 40 Syndrome. It almost always happens at the same time on every trip. It's a point when we've been out for a really long time. And we also have a long way to go. And things are going to get a lot harder—and more dangerous, too. Therefore I need all my physical and mental energy to be focused on the task. Day 40, whether I like it or not, is entering survival mode. Any thought of home, family, or my other life only saps more energy. I am no longer a dad or a husband; I am just a guy trying to get to the North Pole.

Ryan's comments the night before were just the slap in the face I needed. As I made my morning audio update, I could feel my spirits lifting as I compartmentalized my life into survival mode.

> Hi, this is Eric calling in on the morning of day 40 of the Last North Expedition. So we've been out here for 40 days. For 40 days, we've been living in this tent. For 40 days, we've been cooking all our meals over our MSR XGK stoves. Putting in our position with the Delorme inReach. For 40 miles, we've been skiing, snowshoeing and struggling . . . or for 40 days, I mean. I was telling Ryan, I'm so tired now that every morning, I kind of mix up one thing, forget to put an insole in, or,

Overleaf: Ryan looks cold as he scouts the path forward.

you know, put my wrong boot liners in, or just something. It just always seems like no matter how hard I try, there's just one little thing that I messed up. It's a little frustrating, but we kind of joke around here that what are the chances, and here the chances are basically like 50-50. Anyway, we had a really good day yesterday. This is due to a couple of things. One, we got into some bigger—well, medium-sized pans, and the pressure in between wasn't as terrible, even though the light was flat, and we were still kind of tripping, and stumbling, and you know, just our normal polar plod. The other reason is the wind died, and so we weren't battling in drift, we were not getting pushed back every time you lift up a foot. So that helped us out a lot, and we're able to make really good miles, which was just a relief. Today we're hoping to get to our next big, huge, goal, which is the 87th parallel. We're 11 miles from that. Hopefully we don't run into any crazy ice, which we inevitably will, which can just be soldiering. But, uh, we're optimistic as always. Yeah, so 40 days. This is a tough point in the expedition, because we still have a long ways to go, but the finish line is in sight. So it's tough to manage that mentally. We have to really double down, because this is where the trip actually gets harder than it even has been, if you can believe that. But, that's how it goes. That's what we signed up for, and the visibility as of right now is decent, so that's always a positive. Thank you so much for tuning in. I hope you were enjoying Earth Day yesterday, and got out and did something to help protect and enjoy the planet. Thanks so much for following along. Always remember it's cool to be cold. Think snow.

Later that night, after another long day on the ice, the two of us had reason to celebrate. We had knocked out another 13.6 miles and had indeed crossed our first big goal. We were above the 87th parallel. So the two of us munched on one of the bags of cheese puffs we had brought to celebrate. I was so hungry that I tore open the bag and licked the

Fighting forward

inside. I realized that we were going to have to change something in our approach if we were going to be successful. We were 180 miles from our goal, and if we were lucky, we had 12 days left to get there. Our base-camp manager, Elizabeth, had been continually harrying Kenn Borek Air to give us two more days on the ice. Right now it sounded like they might be open to it, but if we didn't start knocking out some serious mileage, they very well could stick with the original deadline. The main pillar of our argument for getting more time on the ice is that we were going to make it to the pole. We would have to average a little over 15 miles a day moving forward to make it within the small window offered to us.

> With the sun up continually, the concept of a normal day was gone.

It was impossible for us to ski any faster. We were too worn down to start sprinting across the ice. We simply couldn't make more miles by being quicker. So the only way to gain miles was be to spend more time on the ice each day. We could average about one mile per hour, at best.

Ryan working his way forward through a rubble field

The two of us decided that starting the next morning, we would spend 14 to 15 hours skiing each day, instead of the 12 we had been doing. With the sun up continually, the concept of a normal day was gone. We skied long into the evening. While prior expeditions have used a similar strategy, they kept their eight-hour sleep time while expanding their day to 30 hours. And with a narrowing logistics window, we didn't have the luxury of maintaining our same sleep schedule. Our new plan was to wake up, spend two hours prepping for the day, ski for 15 hours, then spend four hours at night cooking and drying clothes before sleeping four hours. It would allow us to cut down on the backward drift that happens every time we stop, and would hopefully increase the mileage we could cover each day. We would have to stretch our already thin fuel and food reserves, but we thought we could make it work. The worst part would be the toll on our bodies; it would be a brutal schedule.

I'll describe what we were about to attempt this way: Imagine the hardest thing that you have ever done in your life. Now imagine doing

Hoarfrost crystals on the ice. The darker the ice, the less safe it is.

that for 10 hours a day in subzero temperatures for 40 days straight. Forty days without a break. Forty days of sleeping in a tent and making your own food. Forty days of relying on your own wits for your survival. Forty days under the crushing weight that every decision you make could have deadly consequences. We have just put in 40 days' worth of supreme effort, and now we were going to double it and halve our sleep.

As we sat in the tent after deciding to lengthen our days, I also thought about lightening our loads. "I think we should toss the gun into a lead. It's just dead weight," I said. "Besides, it's very unlikely that we'll see any more polar bears. We're just too far north." He was silent for a minute as he thought.

"There is no way we're leaving the gun," he said. As always, Ryan is a man of few words. I thought about the energy it would save, and how that would increase our chances of getting to the pole. The gun and shells felt like an anchor in my sled. However, the gun had literally saved our lives once already, and it was definitely prudent to keep it. Still, with our new plan, safety and prudence had been thrown out the window, so why not the gun, too? But I knew we were wasting energy discussing the issue, and it wasn't worth fighting over. We would keep the gun all the way to the pole.

As I sat in the tent the next night, I struggled to keep my eyes open. It had been a long, painful day, but we had covered 17 miles in 14 hours. I hurt all over, and Ryan was complaining about the frostbite sores on his legs. Neither of us had been this tired yet. The weather had been perfect all day, and the ice was pretty good. We still had to avoid some leads, but for the most part we were on large pans that allowed us to keep a straight course. The best part was that no new snow had fallen, so the sleds slid relatively well over the ice. Eating my dinner, I reflected upon my food supply. All of the snacking I had been partaking in was having an effect: I would be lucky to make it to the pole with enough food. Ryan had been better with his supplies and was not looking at running low. I would have to start rationing the next day, which would only make things tougher for my already depleted energy stores. While I struggled to type in our blog post, I allowed myself to have a ray of hope. If the weather stayed good, and our bodies did not break down, we might actually stand a chance of making it—maybe. One thing was certain, though. This was probably going to be my last blog post for a while. Sleep was more important than typing. The picture I attached showed how tired I was. I uploaded it and was asleep in minutes. Even Ryan's snoring wouldn't bother me.

Day 41: Making Hay While the Sun Shines

We added two and a half hours of actual skiing to our day which means that with breaks and camp take down and set up we were outside for 14 hours.

There is no question that we are tired but we have a substantial distance to cover and a very limited time to cover it.

Luckily today, there were no extensive areas of crazy ice and all the leads we came across were frozen enough to cross—although the ice still bowed under our weight.

Crossing some fresh ice, you can tell by the absence of piles of snow.

We got into a good rhythm switching lead position every hour and for the first time of the entire expedition my mind began to wander. I thought about having a cookout and going to the park with Merritt and Maria. Then, I started to wonder what things 'normal' people might be able to accomplish in the time I'd been skiing: drive from Colorado to Minnesota, fly across the country (and back), run several marathons (not me of course) . . .

The light was beautiful for most of the day and it reflected off the snow and lit up the pressured slabs transforming each into sparkling blue crystals.

Distance traveled: 17.0 nautical miles

Day 49. We were only 58 miles from the pole. It was morning, and I was exhausted. We had traveled 118 miles over the past eight days, averaging 14.75 miles per day. Plus we crossed two more parallels. Our berserker run yielded results, but we were a mess. Ryan was struggling to

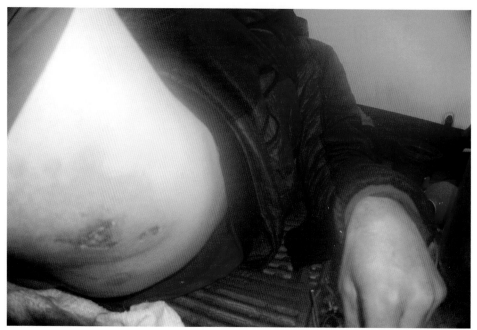

Ryan's legs get worse.

stay awake on the ice each day; several times he had caught himself falling asleep while skiing. The frostbite sores on his thighs were not going away; in fact, they were getting worse. Large, ugly black welts marred his skin, and we had to stop midday to cover them with bandages so he could keep moving forward. They were even worse at night, when they woke him repeatedly whenever he rolled over onto them. Sleeping in the vapor barrier was only worsening the situation.

But he isn't the only one struggling. My rapidly shrinking food stores have conspired to drain my body of all energy. Worse, the extra burden of filming has taken an additional toll. The long days are spirit draining, and it's all I can do to not count the seconds as they slowly pass. For 15 hours, we were out here doing one thing: skiing. At home I could drive from Boulder to Minneapolis in that same time.

> Our life has narrowed to three activities: eat, sleep, ski. Repeat.

Our life has narrowed to three activities: eat, sleep, ski. Repeat. Last night, Ryan was such a mess that the moment we pitched the tent, I told

Moving from one pan of ice to another usually required crossing a pressure ridge.

him to go to sleep while I finished the outside chores of cutting snow blocks and securing the tent. He was out cold in less than three minutes, and only woke to eat, then passed back out. As a team we were functioning well, but this pace couldn't continue much longer. Ryan's gaunt face was a reflection of mine. Both of us were starting to look like POWs. Our ribs were starting to poke out, and our bodies were beginning to consume muscle mass for fuel.

Luckily, the weather gods are again smiling down on us. During the past eight days, we have been blessed with mostly clear skies, warm temperatures (minus 20), no fresh snow, and at times a relatively stable drift that has pushed us mostly eastward but not south. If the weather had turned against us, I don't think we could have kept up the pace. Our spirits were just too fragile. A bad day would break what little willpower and momentum we had left. Maybe the worst part for me was the fact that we were on the ice so long each day that my Nokia would run out of

Overleaf: The beauty of the Arctic is breathtaking.

A lunch break at minus 30

juice after 12 hours, leaving me with three hours of silence and only my thoughts to keep me company.

Survival had become the driving force in our lives: everything we do is designed to be as efficient as possible in order to conserve energy. Even filming had become a chore. In the tent each "night," we struggled to complete the most basic of tasks. When Ryan called in our audio update this morning, I heard hope in his voice as he recounted the polar bear tracks we had come across (thank God we still had the gun) along with all of the other issues we were dealing with. The end might really be in sight.

Hey, good morning, it's Ryan calling in for Last North Expedition, and I think we're on day 50. It maybe 49. Forty-nine slash 50. We can't really decide any more. Uh . . . you ever have one of those days when you've been skiing for like a hundred-and-twenty-plus miles for the past eight days with about four hours, five hours of sleep each night? Then you

Polar selfie

know how you just suddenly hit the wall when you've been redlining those few days? That's how I was yesterday. We were about three-quarters of the way into our day—which is almost, you know seven at, eight at night—in the morning, and . . . just, just really hit the wall. I mean, dehydrated, super tired, the light has been really flat, so it's hard to navigate again, and it was really, it was really difficult yesterday. And, as often that me and Eric come together, we both recognize that I was, you know, dropping fast. And so we made a good plan, like we've done with all the other stuff for gear or time or fuel or anything and . . . you know, just like adapted. So when we finished our day, it was great that I was able to catch some extra sleep, even 45 minutes, before dinner,

Overleaf: A rare moment of celebration on the ice

Eric and Ryan had to be on constant alert to not break their skis when crossing uneven terrain.

which helps huge, a huge amount. Eric really took up the lion's share of the tent work last night, cooking and doing things while I could catch some extra sleep. So that was awesome, and I feel rejuvenated this morning. And we're, we're psyched because we made 89 degrees, yesterday—uh, eighty-nine-O-one. We are officially in the last degree, so we're going to get out and do our best today. One of the funny things is we're beating our head against the wall, you know. It's hard; we're tired, hungry. It was terrible visibility yesterday. We're like, just skiing along trying to make distance, and then what do we come across but massive polar bear tracks, like going exactly our bearing. We were skiing next to this track for a while, and it was going the direction we were going. So we're like thinking, Awesome. Besides all the other stuff we have to look out for, there's a polar bear that's walking the same direction ahead of us. So that was kind of funny, we had to put that into our daily issues to deal with it. But, we never saw it, thankfully. We got to the tent and had a good night, and now it's ready to go this morning. We are just finishing up breakfast stuff and water, and we're about hit this ice and get going now. So stay tuned now for the next few days, and hopefully we get really close to our objective. There's only one last short-term goal left. So thanks for following along, we will be back with more news tomorrow. Thanks.

I was a bit more cynical, but as we ticked off the miles, I was beginning to allow hope to creep into my subconscious. We might actually reach the pole after all. Yesterday morning, on day 48, while I was inventorying my food, I had what I would call a polar miracle. I had mistakenly packed five more breakfasts, unknowingly. I almost started crying at my good fortune. I wouldn't have traded those meals for a million dollars. Knowing we only had four days left on the ice and being able to increase my caloric intake was huge. As I sat in the tent, eating my double helping of food, I was able to smile. We had four days to reach our

> We had taken all of the abuse that the Arctic ice pack has thrown at us and survived.

goal; if we could keep our miles where they had been for the past week, we would reach the pole. We will have completed one of the hardest endeavors on the planet: an unsupported expedition to the North Pole. Ryan would enter into a select group of explorers, and I would have my third successful trip on the ice—more than any other American in history. As I packed my gear and got ready to head out, a smile crept across my face. We had taken all of the abuse that the Arctic ice pack has thrown at us and survived. Over the past eight days, we had accomplished something that just a few weeks ago seemed impossible. I was in the middle of one of the most stunning places on the planet. Things were looking up; we were going to make it.

And that's right when everything goes to shit.

Overleaf: Crossing large cracks next to open water

Chapter 8

A Sinking Ship

Coordinates: 89.27 degrees north, 44 miles to North Pole

By the time we pitched our tent on day 49, we had covered another 17.18 miles. But we had paid dearly for each of them. The 15 hours we spent on the ice had left the two of us so physically and emotionally drained that the simple act of setting up the tent at the end of the day seemed overwhelming. The good news is that we were now only 44 miles (hopefully) from the North Pole.

We spent the day traveling through a whiteout, struggling to find the path of least resistance. The ice was decent for the most part—larger pans with distinct, crossable pressure ridges. But on several occasions, we got stuck in a quagmire of hummocky drifts. Unable to see, we wound back and forth for what seemed like several hours before finally breaking free. On our last shift before lunch, it felt like I was going around in circles. To make matters worse, we also encountered a very large set of polar bear tracks again, heading in roughly the same direction as us.

This was a bear that was tracking on our exact same path.

Over the past few weeks, I had completely forgotten about polar bears. I had assumed that the tracks we saw earlier were a chance encounter. Just bad luck. An anomaly. The ones the other day a fluke. But these fresh tracks proved otherwise. This was a bear that was tracking on our exact same path. Was it waiting for us behind the next pressure ridge? The footprints were a grim reminder of our position on the food chain. Worse, seeing a polar bear this far north, while not completely unusual, only means that it has come a long, long way in search of food. The fact that there was at least one very large bear searching for food somewhere

Left: Skiing on the edge of a fresh lead. The middle was still open water.

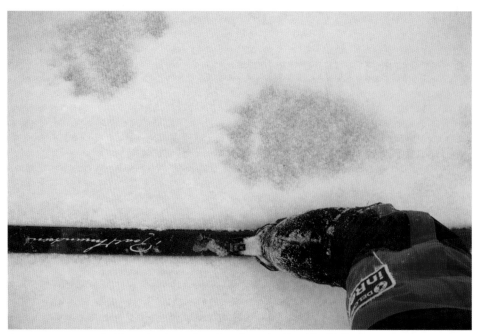

An uncommon sight: polar bear tracks close to the North Pole

just beyond our limited field of vision made both of us nervous. The two of us stopped, and while Ryan filmed the tracks, I got out the gun to oil it and make sure it was in good order. We might need it again soon.

Knowing that there was a bear out there was nerve-wracking, but what really put me on edge was the fear that there might be open water ahead of us. It's a simple equation: Polar bears eat seals. Seals need open water, and therefore leads. So if there's a polar bear hanging around, most likely there is open water, too. If this one was heading north, I worried that he could smell open water ahead of us. It was a bad omen so close to the end. We just need the ice to hold for three more days. As we worked our way forward, I dreaded seeing any cracks or hint of open water emerging from the horizon ahead of us. I didn't know how much more we could take. I just wanted to be done.

As usual, Ryan and I alternated leading, but toward the end of the day he was struggling to keep moving. The sores on his hips and legs had robbed him of valuable sleep over the past few weeks, and he was paying

Right: Polar bear tracks: never a good sign

Ryan navigates through yet another large pressure ridge.

the price. Exhaustion was etched on his face, and he could barely keep his eyes open while skiing. I felt for him, but this was no time to let our guard down. I encouraged him to eat more, even though we were almost out of food, and keep going. I admired him for his perseverance and resolve. Toward the end of the day, the weather started to change. A wind from the north kicked up. Something was coming. I could only hope it would pass over us quickly.

Sitting in the tent, I managed to get a call through on the satellite phone to Maria back home. It felt good to hear her voice as she updated me on her life. But quickly I began to tire of the conversation. I was numb to the details of life in Boulder. It became a sudden intrusion into my singular struggle for survival on the ice. Anything but skiing, sleeping, or eating was an unwelcome distraction compared with the life-and-death struggle we were facing. The harsh realization was that every minute I spent on the phone with my wife was one less minute I could be sleeping. Maria could sense the change in my voice. "Are you even listening to me, Eric?" she asked. "No, no I am not. I don't have time for this right now," I told her. She was furious, and for the next minute she shared her feelings with me. It was too much; something in me snapped. "Look, I just don't give a shit right now, OK? I am really just trying to stay alive up here. Stop yelling at me," I shouted into the phone, and then I hung up. Normally I would never hang up on Maria, and an argument like that would keep me awake. But soon after our conversation, I laid back in my sleeping bag and quickly drifted off to sleep. Guilt was not an emotion I could dwell on at the moment.

When the alarm woke me a short four hours later, I struggled to return to consciousness. Lying there, as the sleep reluctantly receded into the recesses of my mind, I thought about the past 10 days. We had slept roughly 45 hours. That meant that over 80 percent of our time was spent working in the tent or skiing over the ice. The insane workload we had embraced had gotten us within striking distance of the pole, but there was no way we could keep this up much longer. Both of us resembled the walking dead. I was shocked that we had made it this far, considering everything that had happened. I reached over and shook Ryan awake, then checked the GPS to see how far we had drifted while we slept. We had moved almost a quarter-mile back south in the four hours we had stopped moving. Even resting we were getting punished.

Looking over my meager rations brought the precariousness of our situation into sharp focus. The five meals I had found two days ago were helping, but in reality, I had two days of full rations left. Then I would be forced to break into my emergency rations. On the plus side, our long hours on the ice, the improving weather, and fuel rationing had actually left us with a surplus of white gas—an impossible prospect, considering that we had almost aborted our journey due to a lack of fuel only two weeks prior.

Overleaf: Close to the end

As I slowly ate my breakfast, I knew we were nearing the end of this ordeal, whether we reached the North Pole or not. Either way, in three days we would have to stop and wait for the plane to pick us up. All we could do was keep heading north and hope our luck would hold out.

As we head out, I could sense a change happening. The weather was turning nasty, with the wind kicking up and the ice seemingly alive underfoot. Visibility was terrible. Within the first hour of leaving our tent, we crossed several large cracks in the ice, using our skis to bridge the gap over the water. We also encountered an active pressure zone, where two sheets of ice were quickly smashing themselves into a pile of rubble. We watched a pile of ice rubble grow to several feet in height in a matter of minutes. Unless you have seen it for yourself, it is hard to describe—or even imagine, for that matter.

We watched a pile of ice rubble grow to several feet in height in a matter of minutes.

Vast, mile-wide sheets of ice slam into each other in staccato movements, cracking five-foot-thick slabs of ice like they're paper thin. Unable to look away, we watch, shivering, our mouths agape at one of nature's most amazing phenomena.

The snow was suddenly soft, after more than a week of being perfect. Within the space of eight hours, the complete nature of the snow had changed, and once again we feel as if we are are dragging the sleds through sand. The scales of luck that had recently been tilted in our favor have, unfortunately, swung against us. The Arctic Ocean, I am reminded, is no place for optimism.

Three hours in, as I was skiing, I suddenly felt the ice give out underfoot. Due to the drifting snow, I had unknowingly skied out onto a section of thin ice. As I looked down, I saw my feet quickly disappear under the water. Immediately, my reflexes kicked in. I planted my poles ahead of my body and began to pull my submerged skis slowly out of the water. Within a few seconds, my right leg was free, and I was able to lever my left leg out. I moved forward quickly, heading for a thicker piece of ice where I know I would be safe for a moment. I could feel my heart beating as I rubbed snow over my legs to draw the moisture out. I had sunk up to my shins in a

New ice smashed to rubble. You can tell how new it is by its thinness.

matter of seconds. Ryan was at least a hundred feet behind me. If I had not managed to extract myself, who knows how deep I would have sunk in? The worst part was that I had had no idea I was in trouble until I started sinking. The snow-covered depression I had skied over looked like any of the thousand others I had traversed on this trip. But I knew better. The only times I have ever fallen through the ice were when new snow was blowing and drifting. I had dodged a bullet this time, but with deteriorating weather conditions and increasing physical exhaustion, I would need to be extra vigilant.

Over the next few hours, the ice began to progressively degenerate. Pressure ridges and pans that were once squeezed tightly together by unseen force were now relaxed and separating. Where a few days ago the surface had been a relatively solid pack of ice, it was now a fractured morass loaded with hazards. Moving through it, I felt like a soldier trudging new territory, ever nervous about where the next land mine will be. Except in my case, I am dodging thin ice and open water. Previously on

Overleaf: Conditions deteriorating rapidly

this trip there was open water, but nothing to this level. The thinning of the sheet has caused the ice to break apart much more regularly. Several times we were forced to jump from one block of ice to another, trailing a rope to cross a large gap. Leaping onto a floating block of snow-covered ice is just another instant in a series of increasingly life-threatening situations we kept encountering.

It was like a perverse version of the childhood game of lava—the game where you jump from a piece of furniture or playground equipment to another, and if you land on the ground you get burned. Except this time, failing to land safely could result in death. There is this moment of uncertainty as everything is shifting underfoot, but you take a deep breath, and jump. Once we got to the other side, we pulled the two sleds over the open water. Other times, we use the two sleds lashed together side by side as a bridge. Overall, it is an exhausting and time-consuming way to travel.

> As I labored to pull the drysuit up and over my boots, I thought about the absurdity of our situation.

Right before lunch, we skied up to a large, 100-foot-wide gap in the ice. Black salt water disappears into the horizon to the east and west. The only way across will be to don our big orange Gumby suits and swim. We knew swimming was a possibility, but so far we had gotten lucky, skiing and snowshoeing around larger gaps. As I labored to pull the drysuit up and over my boots, I thought about the absurdity of our situation. Here I am, in the middle of ice as far as I can see, it's minus 20 degrees, and I am voluntarily deciding to go for a swim. Granted I will be entombed in an awkward and bulky waterproof-membrane drysuit that's similar to an open-water-sailing survival suit. Hopefully it will not leak, but still, I am less than 50 miles from the North Pole, getting into the water to swim between two sheets of ice. I can only hope that the polar bears are nowhere nearby.

As I slid into the water, I rolled over on my back. The air trapped inside the suit made me fairly buoyant, so sinking was the least of my worries. I do not feel any water seeping in through the numerous seams and stitching I had patched back in Resolute Bay. If my clothes get wet here in the middle of this rotten ice, I will be become hypothermic in a matter of

Hopping from one floating block of ice to the next. It was so unstable, the sleds had to be pulled over the water.

minutes and most likely die not long after. Before I got into the water, I slung a loose loop of rope over my left shoulder and under my right arm so that, once on the other side, I could pull the two sleds over together with Ryan riding on top. The fact that I was the one swimming was not debated. Ryan's drysuit is a tighter fit, and it takes longer for him to get in and out. Also he is physically worn out and less experienced at swimming leads. As much as I would prefer otherwise, it's the logical choice for me to swim. As I slowly paddle myself through the water, I roll over every few minutes to make sure I'm headed in the right direction.

It's hard to describe what I was doing while swimming. The technique is makeshift at best—lying on my back with my head toward the opposite shore, legs flailing in a froglike kicking motion, arms paddling windmill-style through water and thin ice. This lead has a thin film of frozen ice on top of it, and I have to break my way through, leveraging my torso on top, and then letting my body weight break a path. Ryan is filming me, and shouting encouragement as I swim. After 15 minutes, I finally

Eric hauls Ryan across open water on the sleds rafted together.

cross the 200-foot gap and reach the other side. Now came the hardest part: getting out. I flipped over to my front, and then crawled along the ice edge to a low point. There I took my polar picks—basically two handles with sharp points at the ends of a 30-inch lanyard—from around my neck and used them to pull myself up. Luckily, the thin ice of the lead had a few larger ice chunks frozen in that created a more stable surface, and I was able to drag my way up and slide toward the multiyear ice of the floe edge several feet away. Once I was clear of the water, I remained on my back for a second to catch my breath. My heart was pounding in my ears: that was one hell of a workout. Then I stood up, untied the rope, and pulled Ryan across the lead. "That looked fun," he said as he got close.

For the rest of the day, we struggle to find our way through the ever-worsening ice. I broke through again, but only up to my foot. Ryan broke through as well, and I had to swim two more leads and pull him across. By the time we decided to pitch the tent, both of us were a wreck. The constant stress of the moving ice, coupled with the appearance of larger amounts of open water, has left us mentally and physically fatigued.

We had somehow crossed another 14.1 miles, and were now halfway through the final degree. We were less than 26 miles from the pole, but again something needed to change—these 15-hour berserker days would kill us. We didn't have enough food, and our bodies could no longer sustain that level of effort. We needed to get more rest. It wasn't really a decision; we simply had no other choice. We had to change our travel schedule.

By the time we decided to pitch the tent, both of us were a wreck.

This time, we will travel for six hours, pitch the tent to melt snow, eat, take a quick nap, then knock out another six hours, stop for a meal, sleep for a few hours, and then repeat. Basically, we would do temporary bivouacs instead of setting up full-blown camps. With the sun never setting, we would create our own days. By traveling this way, we thought we should be able to put in close to 12 hours on the ice during a traditional 24-hour day while eating the same amount of food. We hoped that the shorter days would help us recharge our depleted bodies with sleep and sustenance. Mentally, not being on the ice for such long stretches would be a huge boost, too. Eating one real meal per shift would be tough, but we had to keep moving. The window of time was closing. Either we would make the pole or we wouldn't. Only one thing was certain: We were not going to give up. For the first time of the entire trip, I allowed a bit of hope to seep into my consciousness. If we could maintain our pace in the deteriorating conditions, we would make the pole in two days. It would be hard, but the end was in sight.

After four hours of sleep, I groggily awoke in my sleeping bag. Everything hurt all over; there was not a single part of me that was not aching. I wonder, how is it possible to have sore muscles after 50-plus days of this? I swallowed four ibuprofen—vitamin I, as we affectionately called it—and set about prepping for breakfast. Speed was of the essence. Every minute we lingered here, we were drifting south, away from the pole. Within an hour and a half, the two of us were outside getting ready for our first six-hour shift of the final mad dash to the finish line. I figured we would need to put in four six-hour blocks of skiing to make it to the pole. If we could average five miles for each block, we would make it to the pole

Navigating the maze

in the two days we had left to us, but that is contingent on nothing else going wrong.

We were only 40 minutes in when the exhaustion hit me. I struggled to stay focused and keep up with Ryan. My legs felt like lead as I wove through the ice. I was famished, and ate half of an energy bar in an attempt to get a little nourishment into my body, but even that had little effect. I turned up my music, and ate the second half of the bar, hoping that my body could convert the nutrients into muscle movement. It helped a little, but it was going to be a long day.

All around us, the ice has turned to shit. It's like someone pulled the plug, and all of the ice that was previously held together was now spreading apart. Pressure ridges that were once compressing now had five-foot gaps of water running down the middle. Everywhere the ice cracked as it pulled apart. Nothing was stable. Worse, the pans seemed smaller, so there were more decisions to make when route-finding. I was constantly on edge, nervous about falling in and fearful we wouldn't make it to the

The author swims across a large lead.

pole. As I struggled through the broken ice, I felt like Indiana Jones in the movie where he runs across the disintegrating bridge: each step looks like his last, yet he keeps going, maybe to his doom, or salvation. The leads we encountered were dangerously thin, forcing us to take time-consuming detours east and west to keep heading north. Often I thought we were headed in the right direction, only to find we were instead surrounded on three sides by open water. To make things worse, the sky was overcast and the light was flat, creating whiteout conditions. Trying to find our way forward was torturous. When Ryan took the lead, I relaxed only slightly, as the anxiety of what might lie ahead weighed heavily on me.

Taking over from Ryan, and now several hours into the day, I paralleled a large lead for 15 minutes. I had my Sony POV camera on, and I was narrating about the conditions when I looked down and saw fresh polar bear tracks, maybe a day old—heading in the exact same direction we are. I unleashed a string of expletives in frustration. It's not so much that there's a polar bear somewhere out here, it's that it's a really big polar bear, who is probably hungry and is walking the exact same direction we are going. "Is it following us?" I wondered out loud.

I yelled back at Ryan to check his flare, and then snap a few pictures. I stop to check the gun, and continue skiing again. The lead narrows to a small, slushy gap. Seeing the bear tracks wears at my already thin nerves. At what point does all this become too much? I start to talk out loud to hide my fear. "We don't mean you any harm, old man bear. We just want to go to the North Pole, and then you'll never see us again!"

When we make it to our first bivouac, or bivy 1 as we call it, I pull out the GPS unit. It shows we have knocked out 4.5 miles and are now 21.5 miles from the pole. Much as I feared, we are slowing down. In the tent I always feel better, but my mental resolve is crumbling fast. Emotions that I have kept restrained so well in the past week are finally surfacing. The two of us scarf down some food and fall asleep for a quick nap. As I doze off, a terrifying thought pops into my head. What if the pole is nothing but open leads of water? What if this effort is for naught? What if we fight our way there and find the final stretch blocked by ocean?

When we woke up three hours later, I managed to place a quick phone call to Maria back home. My voice was quivering as I gave her the update. Completely gone was the argument from a few days ago, replaced by exhaustion and fear. I tried not to cry as I told her that we may not make it, that all of our effort and struggle was for nothing. "Just keep going, Eric, hopefully you make it, but keep going. Regardless of what happens, I am proud of you," she told me. In tears, I hung up the phone and started to pack up my gear. I just want to get home. I want to see my family again.

Six hours later, we were in bivy 2. The bad ice from the first six-hour block turned out to just be an appetizer before the main course. The last stretch of ice was horrendous. Everywhere we turned there was chaos. Pans of ice were continually in motion. All around us, we could hear sheets of ice grinding together or tearing apart. I fell through the ice twice, not sinking too deep, and Ryan went through once. I had to don the drysuit three times to ferry us across dangerous leads, and Ryan had to suit up once to crawl across one

Everywhere we turned there was chaos.

Ryan's sled wedged between two blocks of ice

partially frozen lead. The worst was when I swam across a gap of ocean about 100 feet wide and realized I had forgotten my polar picks. The ice "shore" was nearly two feet high, and I struggled to pull myself out of the water, repeatedly falling back into the ocean. I couldn't get up. It was too high. Several times I was close to getting enough leverage, but my strength gave out and I slipped back down. These are the situations that they find people dead in, I thought, before Ryan called out from atop the sleds. "The ice gets lower to the left."

My heart was racing and my breathing was labored. I had been in the water for close to 15 minutes now, and I was beginning to worry that I may never get out. I focused on moving my body along the ice edge, guiding myself hand over hand until there was only a foot-high ledge. This, I feel, is the last effort my body has left. After this, I will be too tired to get out. I lifted my hands out of the water and up onto the ice, digging into the deep snow to form handholds. Then, in one fluid motion, I kicked my legs and pulled up with my arms, trying to get as high as possible before squirming my way out of the water, much like a seal exiting the ocean. I rested for a second on my hands and knees in the snow, thinking, I could have died. That was close. Standing up, I reached for the rope that connected to the two sleds and Ryan. It's not there. Frantically, I searched the snow and quickly realized my mistake. It had slipped off my body and was floating 25 feet away. Ryan and the sleds were stranded on the other side. But without a second thought, I slid back into the ocean, even though my muscles were still shaking with fatigue.

By the time we were both on the correct side of the water, I was destroyed. Physically the crossing took a toll, but mentally I was shaken even worse. I almost didn't make it out alive, and I knew it. It was all I could do to keep moving forward. Luckily Ryan was able to take the lead next and give me a much needed break. I felt like I was coming apart at the seams, and an hour in second position could mend my frayed psyche. By the end of the day, officially day 51, we had covered 11.85 miles, were 19 miles from the pole, and were at 89.68 degrees north.

When we awoke three hours later, the efforts of the previous 18 hours, both physically and emotionally, still weighed heavily upon me. The weight of so much uncertainty and fear is an unbearable burden. I had allowed myself to think the ice would improve, and like always, it did the exact opposite. It got worse. Way worse. Nothing seemed to be lining up for us. The little bit of good luck we had had on days 40 through 49 had blown away like so many other of our dreams. As I called in the audio update, I could barely keep it together enough to get words to come out, and in the middle I actually started crying.

> Hey, this is Eric calling in. I just want to give you a quick
> update. We're nineteen-point-one miles away from the pole
> and things are really, really difficult. There's water every-
> where, there's leads everywhere, and broken ice everywhere.
> The pans are small. We're just trying not to get stuck in these
> areas that are like peninsulas surrounded by water, having
> to put on the drysuits, and swim quite a bit. It's, it's snow-
> ing, and it's a total whiteout. So I've fallen, fell through twice
> yesterday, once with one foot, once with both feet. I think

Ryan went in. We just punched through at random occasions, because you just can't see anything. Progress is just really slow, because we're just trying to just find a way through, we're just veering backwards at times just to get through some of the stuff, and it's just crazy all the things we have to do. Uhm, it's just crazy. So . . . we're going to keep going . . . and see what happens. Thanks for following along. We still remain optimistic, and are persevering toward our goal, and are working well together . . .

I knew we were close, so close; if we just had one more day. I e-mail Elizabeth and ask her to see if Kenn Borek Air would be open to letting us have one more day on the ice. We are so tired and our food is so limited that there is no way we will be able to cover 19 miles in one day. It was early in the morning back in the real world—1 a.m. It looked like today we should be able to knock out two of our six-hour travel shifts. If we got lucky and averaged eight miles per shift, that would leave us only three or four miles from the pole. One more day would get us there.

The fact that the end was near was terrifyingly wonderful. It was officially day 52, and I knew we had a gargantuan task ahead of us, one filled with stress and pain. But at the end we were going to be picked up and flown out of here—provided there was good enough ice to land a plane on to pick us up. If we had to travel back out of this morass we'd been struggling through, things were going to get very dangerous. I was into my last full day of rations, and Ryan was not far behind. We had enough fuel to melt snow, but the prospect of having to knowingly put ourselves in more danger to find better ice was one best not thought about. We would need food to fuel further travel, and we would have none. The emergency rations were designed for five days staying in one spot, burning minimal calories, not skiing.

Within minutes of heading out, we ran into our first issue. A vast swath of barely frozen ice extended as far as I could see. There was no way

> The fact that the end was near was terrifyingly wonderful.

Bringing a sled across a fresh crack in the ice

around it. If it was earlier in the trip, we would have just camped for the night and crossed it at first light. But that was not an option now. Ryan was in lead, and I tried to steel my nerves with his confidence. Crossing these floating chunks of ice is a death sentence. Fall between them and there is no way out. Ryan unhooked from his sled and tested the ice in between. For a few feet, to a large car-size chunk of ice, it is stable. I exhaled a huge sigh of relief. Maybe we could cross after all. Ryan's persistence paid off, and it allowed me enough leverage on my emotions to jump-start my confidence again. We unhooked from the sleds, hopping from one chunk of ice to the next, towing the floating sleds behind. It took us 15 minutes to cross an area that we could have skied across in two. Over the next six hours, we struggle forward. We never gave up, but we were confronted with so many seemingly insurmountable obstacles that it seemed crazy to keep going. By the time we pitched the tent for our nap, the two of us were struggling to stay upright. We had knocked out 8.03 miles and were now only 11.14 from the pole. How, I do not know. Crawling into the tent, I didn't even bother to get my sleeping bag out.

It's only minus 20 outside with the sun shining, and inside, in my gear, I'm not even cold, just exhausted. I just curled up on the sleeping pad and blacked out within a minute.

Waking two and a half hours later, I saw Ryan was also sprawled out on his sleeping pad. Neither of us even bothered taking off our boots. I reached over and shook Ryan awake. He groggily looked at me, sat up, and started rummaging in the food. He turns back to me, saying, "Bad news man, the coffee is almost out, and you know what they say?" I looked across at him and asked in mock earnest, "No, what's that?" He smiled and said over the roar of the stove, "When the coffee's out, it's time to go home." I agreed. It is time to go home. We quickly consumed the little food we had and set back out again.

What followed was quite possibly the most Herculean effort of the entire trip. The ice was still terrible, route-finding was nearly impossible, both of us broke through several times, and were forced to swim. We just kept moving. The closer we got to the pole, the less either of us wanted to stop. Some unknown reservoir of energy deep inside of us was tapped, and we found the willpower to keep moving forward. Each time we looked at our GPS, it

> What followed was quite possibly the most Herculean effort of the entire trip.

showed us getting closer and closer to the end. By the time we stopped, we were only 3.5 miles from the pole. Both of us wanted to keep going, but we had logged over eight hours on the ice. We were zombies. As I crawled into the tent, I looked at the GPS. We were at 89.94 degrees north. We had crossed 416 miles of Arctic ice. Just over the horizon was the end of this nightmare.

Waking up three hours later, I could hear the ice breaking apart not far from our tent. The sound of ice cracking is not the most pleasant of sounds at any time, but when you're lying in a sleeping bag in the middle of a morass of broken ice, it is even worse. All I could think was that the ocean was desperately trying to swallow us up. We were not wanted here.

Overleaf: Ryan crossing a lead that did not break, even though it was cracking underfoot

I could hear the message loud and clear, and I wasn't going to stay longer than I had to.

The difference in the quality of the ice compared with my last expedition here four years ago was shocking. Nothing was stable; the entire area around the pole seemed to be disintegrating all at once. It reminded me more of what we dealt with in 2006, when Lonnie and I were here during summer. If this is the future of the North Pole in the age of climate change, then we are lucky to have made it this far. With the polar melt starting earlier each year, I seriously doubt anyone will ever get this close on a land to pole trip again.

As Ryan fired up the stove to melt some water, I saw we had an e-mail from Elizabeth. We would get one more day. Our final push had convinced Kenn Borek to wait a little longer. As I put my remaining bits of food into the pot for a quick meal, I listened to Ryan as he called in our audio update. He sounded exhausted.

> Hey, it's Ryan calling for Last North Expedition. I'm in the tent here, about a little over just three and a half nautical miles from the North Pole. We've been at it for a super long time, doing these six-hour walks with a little rest in between, and we did a really long eight and a half or eight-point-nine miles on our last shift. Even though we're really close, we just thought it best to put up our tent, get some lunch, get out of this wind. It's very cold and windy today, so that we decided to regroup and be ready to do this last bit here up to the, hopefully to the pole. We've been, uh, it's been a challenge, all the way, every, every bit, just doesn't let up at all. Since we called in last, we've probably swam I don't even remember how many times. But, many times with the drysuits on, swimming leads, uhm, catamaraning our sleds, crawling across, across leads, even jumping across leads and onto floating ice. At one point we were both on a big ice raft with our sled and we were floating around in the middle of the lead. It's just been pretty crazy, and the conditions are really flat light still, but it makes it hard to ski on the surface.

But it doesn't matter, because we're just trying to problem-solve and getting through all this; we're very close now. We're about to zip up all of our gear here and get out and find our direction to the pole. So we'll be calling in shortly, hopefully with good news. Stay tuned and you can follow our progress . . . Alrighty, we'll back soon. Thanks a lot for following.

I had been hesitant about stopping when we set up the tent. The wind was picking up, and clouds were rolling in. Bad weather and low visibility could dramatically affect our chances of reaching the pole. But stopping was a necessary evil. We didn't have enough energy to keep going, even though every minute we slept narrowed our weather window further.

A few hours later, I woke with start. I had overslept. Somehow, in my overly fatigued state, I had set my alarm incorrectly and lost nearly two hours of travel time. The speed record had long since vanished from our grasp, but every minute counted out here when all of our reserves—both physical and mental—were dwindling dangerously low. After eating, the two of us packed up our gear. We were almost finished. If we got lucky and found good ice ahead of us, we could be at the pole in a little over two hours. Besides reaching the pole, we also needed to find a large enough piece of ice for the plane to land on to extract us from all this chaos. While they can land on less, Kenn Borek pilots generally require a 1,600-foot swath of flat multiyear ice. We hadn't seen a pan of ice that large in weeks. Getting to the North Pole, it seemed, could be easier than getting home.

Getting out of the tent, my fears were realized. The wind had picked up and the light was flat. By the time Ryan and I started skiing, the wind was blowing directly in our faces, and the horizon had disappeared completely. Whiteout is the worst. We were working so hard that our goggles fogged up, making it almost impossible to distinguish any difference in surface conditions. Slowly, Ryan made his way through a relatively flat

> We didn't have enough energy to keep going, even though every minute we slept narrowed our weather window further.

Crossing a bridge of ice before it turns the wrong direction

swath of ice. Navigation was nearly impossible, as we can't see anything and we can't raise our faces enough to look up due to the wind. Our progress was not much faster than it was on day 1, even though our sleds were considerably lighter. Mother Nature seemed furious that we had the audacity to attempt reaching the pole.

We were at it no more than 20 minutes when I saw a long, thin gun-metal gray line on the horizon, the reflection of black open ocean on the far edge of a lead. Ryan, skiing in lead, had been focused on route-finding and hadn't yet noticed the daunting obstacle. Of course, I think to myself. Of course there would be another lead. A few minutes later, I saw Ryan stop, then catch sight of the lead. His shoulders dropped and his posture sagged under the burden of all the chaos. I could tell what he was think-ing, because I was thinking the exact same thing. How much more can we take? When will it stop?

As we got closer, I could tell that we were facing one of the largest open-water leads of the entire trip. It looked like the Mississippi River. I could barely see the opposite side through the swirling snow. Ryan looked defeated, his head hung low. He had expressed hope in the tent that the final stretch would be relatively easy; the Arctic would finally give us a break. Unfortunately having hope up here is dangerous. It's a feeling best left on land.

"It's just too much man, I don't know if I can keep going," he said to me. I could hear the tears in his voice. Finally, on the last day of our expedition, the rigor of the Arctic Ocean has broken my partner. He had persevered through injury, lack of sleep, incessant stress, and a moody teammate with his usual calm. But finally he was crying uncle.

Luckily I had had my worst moment a day and a half prior, tired and exhausted and ready to throw in the towel. I, too, had assumed the ice was going to get better, and when it didn't, I was shattered. It was a tough lesson to learn on day 51 but a good reminder of my overall survival strategy for polar travel. Always assume conditions will be terrible.

> Hoping for something that will never happen can destroy a person.

Ryan, unfortunately, had started today with high hopes. Only a few miles. Easy travel. Our natural inclination was to be optimistic and hopeful. But those types of thoughts are delicate, and dangerous. Hoping for something that will never happen can destroy a person.

But, as was so common on this trip, when one of us was down, the other was up. When I had cracked two days ago, Ryan stepped up and kept us moving. Now it was my turn. "Listen, man, we can do this. We are so damn close, nothing is going to stop us," I told him. "I will swim across and pull you over to the other side."

As I pull on the drysuit, I could understand how he felt. Many times on this trip I just wanted to quit. It seemed that the deck was stacked against us, yet we kept moving north. Today we would keep moving and, hopefully, we would reach the pole. If we didn't, it wouldn't be from a lack of effort.

Thirty minutes later, the two of us were on the other side of the lead. I had swum across and then hauled Ryan and the sleds over. It was a tough swim, but we were both across the obstacle. When I looked at our GPS, I was surprised to see that we were farther south than when we started

The ice breaking up around Eric and Ryan

crossing the water. We had actually drifted backwards. The fierce wind was causing the ice to drift faster than at any other time on the trip. Every step was going to be hard-won.

Over the next seven hours, the two of us engaged in a pitched battle for our lives. It felt like every piece of shit that the Arctic Ocean possessed was thrown in front of us in a pulverized landscape of incessant leads. Every time we got to the other side of a lead, we would be lucky to have 100 yards of solid ice before we were confronted with more crazy ice—a chaotic mix of leads, thin ice, pressure ridges, and floating ice chunks. Navigation was nearly impossible. I was squinting through one eye into the wind, trying to use the sun as a reference point, weaving back and forth to find any sort of stable path.

From that first open-water crossing, I skied in the lead position, offering as much encouragement as possible to Ryan. We didn't stop for our usual hourly snack breaks—not that we had any food to eat, really. At one point, I simply grabbed an extra piece of butter and swallowed it whole. We were engaged in a real-life version of the classic arcade game *Frogger*. One misstep could lead to death. As we leaped from one block of floating ice to another, a grim resolution set in. We were in a very dangerous situation; there would be no way for anyone but the two of us to extract ourselves from it. We had to find safety out here.

We got lucky at one point and found a singular spot of connected ice between two pans—only to come to more open water and thin ice 100 yards later. For this crossing, I improvised a new strategy that I dubbed fishing. I lay spread-eagle on the rafted sleds, hands extended forward. Ryan tied a rope to the back of our sleds, and then pushed me out toward the far shore. Not having enough momentum to break the thin ice, he "reeled" me in again then "cast" me back toward the far shore. After several attempts, I was able to get onto the ice and then ferry Ryan across.

It's difficult to describe all the effort that went into those last few miles—just stopping to check the GPS meant that we lost valuable progress north. There was never a moment when we thought that we might actually reach the pole—there was always some crazy obstacle blocking our path. But we were getting close, and the visibility improved enough that I could see a large pan in the distance, easily the largest pan of ice in several days. I was dumbstruck. Could our last stretch to the pole be an effortless ski? No. Of course, not. Separating us from it was another large lead. Another lead created the western edge of the massive pan.

It's difficult to describe all the effort that went into those last few miles.

"What's next?" Ryan joked, exhausted. "Are dragons going to pop out of the ice and eat us?" It truly seemed like the Arctic Ocean was trying to devour us once and for all.

I looked at the GPS: we were about three-quarters of a mile from the North Pole. It was just ahead. Would it be in the middle of that flat ice, or would the ice shift enough by the time we crossed the first lead that we would miss it and head directly into another lead? It was hard not to be a tad optimistic, but the reality was that I had a bigger problem to deal with. I had to swim across that lead separating us from salvation.

My drysuit was damp inside as I pulled it on. I had been in and out of the ocean so often today that snow had gotten inside. Everything was damp, actually. The battle we had fought to get here had forced us to abandon all of my steadfast rules of polar safety. Every step was an improvisation. My food was gone, the final remnants of my supplies eaten a few hours earlier when I scarfed down my last pat of lifesaving butter. All I had was a couple of days of emergency rations, barely enough calories for resting in one place. As I lowered myself into the water, the exhaustion of it all hit me at once. I just wanted to be done. I wanted to be safe and not in constant fear for my life. I wanted to be warm, and to eat lots of food. I wondered if I would ever see Maria and Merritt again. And I worried about the ice on the other side of the lead, as the memory of my nearly fatal crossing still haunted me. I didn't want to die, especially this close to the North Pole.

It was a slow process, swimming and breaking ice, but as I pulled myself up the other bank, I could tell it was a beautiful piece of thick multiyear ice. Hallelujah, I mouthed to myself. I quickly pulled Ryan across on the sleds, then wiggled out of my drysuit while he untied the sleds from one another. I checked the GPS again. We had lost one-fifth of a mile crossing the lead due to the southerly drift of the ice. "Hurry up," I snapped at Ryan. It was not my finest moment, but the stress was over-whelming. Too much had gone into this expedition to not reach the pole, and every second we hesitated we drifted south. Surprisingly, our bearing was still good—prior to crossing the lead it was more westerly—but now it veered more to the east, directly into the middle of the large pan. I finally allowed myself to think that we might actually make the pole. I couldn't believe it. We crossed over a small pressure ridge, and the GPS showed we were less than a quarter-mile from the pole.

Ahead of us was a large expanse of relatively flat ice; there were no leads that I could see. I turned to Ryan and said, "We made it, right in front of us is the North Pole. Let's go find it, and then let's get the hell out of here." The two of us unhitched the sleds and dug out our cameras. I had removed the DeLorme transmitter and mine a few hours earlier when they had gotten in the way while climbing out of a lead. I switched on my camera and filmed the two of us as we walked toward the direction of the pole. Ryan had the GPS unit in his hand and began to count off the distance in meters as we got close—20, 18, 16 . . . I couldn't believe how

Arrival at the North Pole!

happy I was. We had gone through hell to get here. I was laughing out loud every time he called out a number—14, 12, 10 . . . I looked over at him as he called out the distances. I could hear the joy in his voice; I was so happy to be able to share this experience with him. Reaching this point was truly the result of our combined effort.

This was likely to be the last time I would ever be here, so I looked around to savor the view—9, 11, 13 . . . I couldn't believe it, we were moving away. "We're going up?" I asked Ryan. "Yeah that's right," he said, looking at the unit. I checked our compass bearings and could tell we were headed in the right direction; the ice was drifting so fast that we were moving faster away from the pole than we were walking toward it. It was fitting; the ice was still trying to defeat us. In the minute it took to check our heading, we had moved close to 135 feet away from our goal. We started toward the pole again. This time we would not stop. One minute later, Ryan started the countdown again as I filmed—5, 4, 3, 2, 1 . . . We were there. The GPS showed 90 degrees north. We were standing on top of the world. The two of us yelled and high-fived. "How does it feel to be here?" I asked Ryan. He looked at me. There was a long icicle hanging from his face mask. I could see myself reflected in his goggles.

Celebrating at the pole

"Holy shit is all I can say," he said. "It feels pretty incredible."

I aimed the camera at the GPS to show our location, and shot pictures I had seriously wondered if I would ever be able to take. So many obstacles had been thrown in our way, yet we had overcome them all. Barely.

We quickly pitched our tent and called for a flight to come get us out. Even though I was exhausted and wanted to do nothing more than to go to sleep, I knew I had to type up a blog post and call home. When I got hold of Maria, I could tell she was a bit miffed at me. "What's wrong?" I asked her.

"Did you know that for two hours, everyone here thought you were dead? We were freaking out," she said. In her voice I could hear the toll this trip had taken on her; it had been hard on her, too. Turns out that when I had taken off my DeLorme transmitter less than a mile from the pole and put it in the sled, I had inadvertently turned it off. While we had been struggling to cover the final 0.7 mile over the past two hours, back home it appeared that we had dropped off the radar. We had stopped transmitting our position. Everyone had thought we fell through the ice and drowned. I apologized profusely and told her how much I loved her before I hung up. It felt good that I would be reunited with her soon—and that I hadn't fallen through the ice and died.

In the tent, Ryan broke out our last can of Pringles, and the two of us snacked on them while dinner cooked. It felt good to be finished; I don't know if we could of have continued much longer. We were at the end of our rope. Best of all, the large piece of ice we were on would support a plane landing. Still, there was one final worry. "How much are you going to eat tonight?" Ryan asked. We had a few of our emergency rations left and not much else. With these conditions, there was no way a plane would fly. We had been delayed eight days at the start; we could easily be stranded for that long now. "I'm going to eat a full meal and worry about it tomorrow." I replied.

We were out of food, but at least we would not have to go searching for a place where we could be evacuated. It seemed like the Arctic gods were finally truly smiling down upon us. We had overcome all they had thrown in our path, and now they would allow us to rest. I posted the blog entry I had been fumbling with for the past hour and finally laid down to sleep. For the first time in a long time, I did not have to set the alarm. It was a wonderful feeling.

Day 53: THE NORTH POLE!

Well, it took 8 hours but we managed to cover the whiteout, windy, leads everywhere, fractured, pressured, thin ice to the North Pole.

We are elated and exhausted—we have nothing left.

I know there were some concerns about InReach tracking for an hour near the pole, but I keep the beacon in a chest pocket on my bibs (and a camera inside my shirt) and they kept getting caught on the edge of leads as I was trying to climb out of the water. It is very scary to be in the water and unable to pull yourself out. Therefore, for the final lead, I took everything out and put it safely in the sled. Sorry to those who were nervous.

If you were watching our progress live, you probably also noticed how much we were moving south—that's because in stopping to put my drysuit on, we would lose up to one quarter mile of progress.

Refueling the plane before takeoff

I will follow up later, but I wanted to thank Maria and Merritt, the two most amazing people in the world (besides my nephews Tyler and Luke).

Yesterday, the government released the National Climate Assessment. Now, I'm not a scientist, but I've spent my life in the snow. I'm seeing climate change firsthand. It's affecting places like the North Pole, where I am now and I'm here because we all need to take notice. Please believe the science, and take action like by joining Protect Our Winters and help them support the EPA standards on power plants, the source of 40% of US carbon emissions.

There's more just like this expedition—reaching the North Pole is not the end of a journey rather the beginning . . .

And the real work starts now.

Think Snow!

Distance traveled: 3.5 nautical miles (in 8 hours)

I woke up 36 hours later. Since we had crawled inside our tent, we had drifted almost nine miles south. The message was loud and clear: we were

Sleds stacked inside the plane between drums of fuel and folded seats

not wanted here, and the ice was rapidly taking us farther away, much like it had been doing the entire trip. I woke once to call in a quick audio update and eat some of the food we still had left. But mostly, all I wanted to do was sleep. The toll of the past two weeks had destroyed me. When we finally awoke, I played a few games of Angry Birds on my phone, listened to some music, and counted the minutes until we could be picked up. My greatest fear was that we would be stuck on this frozen lifeboat for days until the plane could get to us.

In 2005, we had been stuck on the ice for nine long days; sometimes extradition up here can be delayed. If we had to wait that long this time, we might not survive. The weather was not great as I sent in hourly weather reports now that I was awake, and I assumed that the plane wasn't coming. But when the satellite phone rang, it was the Kenn Borek copilot, letting us know they would be landing in 30 minutes. Luckily our pilot was equally concerned about our fate and took a risk on a small weather window. A few

Overleaf: The long-awaited plane

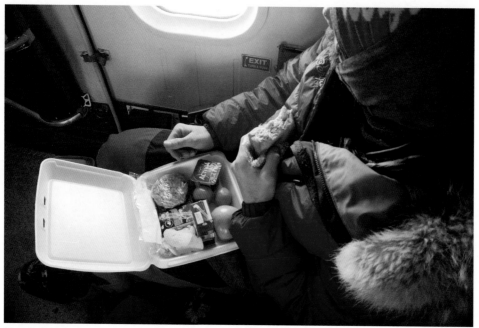

Fresh food

hours earlier we had ventured outside the tent to mark a runway by filling Granite Gear stuff sacks with snow and placing them in a straight line 400 meters out. We also constructed a windsock out of another stuff sack.

Forty-two hours after we stood on the North Pole, the sight of a De Havilland Twin Otter plane landing on the ice was truly amazing. As the plane rolled to a stop in front of us, I felt a moment of sadness. We had been out here for almost two months on our own, seeing another soul only once. I had gotten used to the isolation and total absence of the civilized world. Going back to my life with all of its responsibilities would be tough. Reentry is always hard the first few days. Leaving this magnificent region, with all of its dangerous beauty, is hard. This time, knowing that it's disappearing, made leaving even tougher. We had pushed ourselves to the limit and tested the boundaries of our psyches. Through it all, the two of us had kept traveling north, filming this hidden gem to show the rest of the world. We had dealt with terrible ice, blizzards, polar bears, and a host of other issues in order to stand on top of the world. The thought of leaving it saddened me.

Leaving the North Pole

But then the door of the plane opened, and Troy the pilot stepped out. He had a big smile on his face as he held out his hand and said, "Congratulations on making it, guys. What do you say we take you home?" Then he added, "We had to come get you today; otherwise you would have been stuck here for over a week. The weather is going to get really bad up here." I shook his hand, and in that moment of brief human contact, I was ready to leave. The adventure was over; it was time to go home.

After we loaded our gear and the pilots refueled, we crawled into the plane. The copilot handed us two box lunches each—Elizabeth's handiwork. She knew we would be very hungry. I hugged mine close, waiting for the plane to take off to dig into the fresh food. I pulled out the camera and filmed the two of us sitting in our seats looking at the food. "As soon as we take off, we're gonna be eating this shit, which we're psyched about," I said into the camera. "Oh my God! What is that, a moon pie?" I exclaimed. Ryan replied, "I don't know, but I am super psyched to be on the plane. We're not getting rattled. Just, we don't even know where we're landing, but we're just going to get out of here. That's all." He was

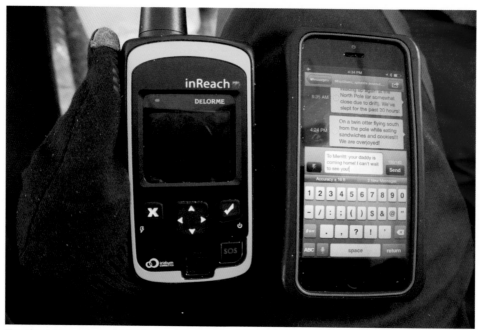

Texting Merritt and Maria

slumped in his chair, with a huge grin on his face. From across the aisle, I replied, "Anywhere but here. The Arctic Ocean is an amazing place, but we're done, man."

The engines roared to life, and we taxied into position at the far end of the pan, the nose facing onto the wind. Troy gunned the engine and we bounced across the ice, rapidly gaining speed. For a moment, it seemed like there wouldn't be enough room. And then we lifted off the ice. Outside the window, I could see what we had crossed. From high up, it looked like shattered glass. There was nothing but shards and fragments of ice continually interspersed with open water. It was like someone had dropped something heavy from high above and broken what was once a solid, beautiful sheet. The North Pole was literally disappearing in front of my eyes. The sun was streaming through the window, and the higher we climbed, I could see blue sky ahead while below the ice disappeared underneath a blanket of clouds. We had escaped just in time.

Looking Forward

Coordinates: 40.01 degrees north, 2,994 miles to North Pole

Once we got off the ice, my only focus was getting home. As the Kenn Borek plane slowly crawled over the Arctic heading south, I allowed my thoughts to turn back to my family. I had been gone for close to 70 days and was looking forward to holding Merritt in my arms and hugging Maria. Once we touched down in Resolute Bay, the two us immediately dove into prepping for the journey home—drying and repacking our gear. Maria had rebooked our flights, and we had a short 24-hour turnaround before leaving Resolute. Of course, there would be one final snafu. A videographer had flown to Resolute to do some additional filming for our Animal Planet documentary. He had rented a snow machine, and we spent several hours shooting a few scenes to supplement our footage. When it was time to head back to the South Camp Inn, the machine wouldn't start up and we had to ski nearly two miles back, limping and sore.

I finally made it back to Boulder on May 13, six days after reaching the North Pole. When I walked through the customs gate and saw Maria and Merritt waiting for me, my heart almost burst. Tears were shed, and for a few minutes Merritt was a little nervous around me. But then everything went back to normal. I ceased to be Eric Larsen, polar explorer, and happily became Eric Larsen, daddy and husband.

When I walked through the customs gate and saw Maria and Merritt waiting for me, my heart almost burst.

For the next few weeks, I focused on spending time with my family, eating (I had lost 10 pounds on the ice), sleeping, and telling the story of the North Pole. Within a few days of getting home, I was working with our production company, sorting through all of the video files we had shot

After everything

on the trip. It was weird to be home and not having to fight the elements every second. Everything seemed to move so fast. Driving in cars was especially weird for some reason—that I could sit and be transported, effortlessly, from one location to another took some getting used to. I was a bit depressed, too. For several years, my primary focus had been the Last North Expedition, and now it was over. Now I lacked focus. Nothing seemed important. The intensity was gone. Eventually I worked through it all, as I had similar experiences returning from prior expeditions.

Most importantly, Maria got pregnant, and on April 14, 2014, our beautiful daughter Ellie Ann Larsen was born. Maria and I cried together when we first held her. She was amazing and perfect, and we dreamed up a variety of family road trips while we nursed Ellie through those first sleepless months. At the same time, Merritt was growing like a weed, learning new words, and trying new things. Every day, I was overwhelmed with love for my kids and Maria. Any of my expeditions still pale in comparison to the adventure of fatherhood.

On December 9, 2015, the documentary *Melting: Last Race to the Pole* debuted on Animal Planet. It was a moment of immense pride for me. The footage we shot was perfect for highlighting the rigors of the trip and—more importantly—the continually deteriorating state of the Arctic ice pack. I have received e-mails and calls from people all over the world who have seen it since its release; hopefully it's helping individuals better understand what's happening in the polar regions of the world and inspiring them to act.

Besides working on the documentary and living a normal life, I went on two other trips with Ryan. It seems that neither one of us got too sick of the other on the ice.

I have had many expedition partners over the years, but none like Ryan. His unparalleled grit and resolve are like no other. He is also my best friend, and there isn't a day that goes by that I don't take that for granted. We don't talk much about the North Pole and the Arctic Ocean, but there are moments when he stops by to have a beer on my back porch and one of us will say, "Remember that one day on the Arctic Ocean . . ." and smile and think, not needing to comment more. The memories of those 53 horrible and amazing days on the ice are a powerful bond that will span the rest of our lives.

> I have had many expedition partners over the years, but none like Ryan.

Only a few months after Kenn Borek plucked the two of us off the ice, the airline announced that it was suspending all air service for North Pole expeditions. The decision shocked the tiny world of Arctic explorers. While most understand why they did it—economically, it just doesn't make sense to them to continue—it still closed a critical service that was needed to complete an over-ice expedition to the pole. North Pole expeditions from the Canadian coast are virtually impossible now, since you can't easily get to Ellesmere Island, and extraction from the ice is also impossible now. Meanwhile, Russia keeps closing Borneo earlier and earlier each year, due to the melting ice. If you want to try to get to the pole from the Russian side, good luck. The logistics are a nightmare, and the ice is usually worse on that side of the cap—it pulls away from the coast, due to currents creating large gaps of open water.

We called our expedition Last North, and as of this writing since our journey no one has successfully gotten to the pole from land—either supported or unsupported. In fact we are the only team to make it since 2010. The ice sheet is just too unstable. The year we made it to the pole was the warmest on record until 2015. As I write this book, all indications are that 2016 will supplant last year and hold the record. This January (2016) was the warmest ever on record. On December 30, 2015, the North Pole was actually warmer than most of the United States—temperatures were almost 60 degrees warmer than normal, and ice was actually melting. Think about that. There was no sunshine; it was pitch black. Yet it was warmer than Chicago on that day.

> These two men fell through the ice just outside Resolute Bay and drowned at a time of year when the ice would normally have been frozen solid.

On April 29, 2015, two well-known veteran polar explorers, Marc Cornelissen and Phillip De Roo, died after setting off on skis to document the thinning polar ice just months after NASA reported that the winter ice cover was the lowest on record. These two men fell through the ice just outside Resolute Bay and drowned at a time of year when the ice would normally have been frozen solid. Their last message was about how warm it was and how unstable the ice was.

The future of the Arctic ice cap is bleak. All indications are that the damage being done is—at least for the short term—irreversible, unless we as a planet come together. Unlike the South Pole, which sits on Antarctica and is designated as an international scientific preserve, the North Pole is in the middle of one of the more contested regions on the planet. Canada, Norway, Russia, Denmark, and the United States all claim a portion or all of the waters of the Arctic Ocean. Part of the issue is that the latest estimates are that over 20 percent of the world's untapped petroleum reserves are located under the Arctic Ocean. Things came to a boiling point in the summer of 2015, when Russia used a remote-control submarine to plant a flag on the floor of the ocean, claiming the area. At the same time, Royal Dutch Shell was trying unsuccessfully to get the first-ever offshore-drilling rigs in place off the Alaskan coast. The race for oil seems to be getting most of the press right now.

Things do look bleak, but there is also hope. Increasingly larger numbers of political and business leaders are realizing that the way forward must be focused on mitigating climate change. When rising sea levels mean that coastal areas like Bangladesh and parts of Florida keep flooding with each full moon, it's hard to ignore the facts. When massive wildfires ravage the Canada and Alaska wilderness, like the ones that burned during the summer of 2015, people can't help but see what's happening. We must support leaders who are proactive on climate issues and want to protect our planet. Environmental groups like the Sierra Club, the World Wildlife Fund, the Union of Concerned Scientists, and 350.org are pushing for change. Together we can fix this issue and leave a better planet for our children.

When I find myself wondering about the future of our wild areas, I sometimes struggle to see beyond the bleak headlines. Then I remember that nothing is static. Being on the ice taught me that. We just have to keep moving forward, regardless of the obstacles in our way. However hopeless things might seem, there is always a solution. We just have to keep looking for it. Like my mantra on the ice . . . Begin with one step.

Notes

Introduction

1. Since this trip is on the ocean all distances are based on nautical miles, approximately 1.2 standard miles.

2. J. Stroeve, M. Serreze, M. Holland, J. Kay, J. Malanik, A. Barrett, "The Arctic's rapidly shrinking sea ice cover: a research synthesis." Climate Change 110: 3–4.

Chapter 1

1. The northernmost island in the world, it is a popular launching point for North Pole expeditions. It has a population of 146 people as of 2006.

2. To be defined as an unsupported expedition, only human power (skis, snowshoes, and sleds) may be used and all supplies must be carried. You are not allowed to have supplies brought to you.

3. A small Inuit village on Cornwallis Island in Nunavut, Canada, it is the traditional staging area for all North Pole attempts from North America.

4. R. Lindsay and A. Schweiger, "Arctic sea ice thickness loss determined using subsurface, aircraft, and satellite observations." Applied Physics Laboratory, University of Washington.

5. Leads are narrow, linear cracks in the ice created when ice floes diverge or shear as they move parallel to each other. The formation of leads is similar to mid-ocean ridges or shear zones that form from Earth's moving tectonic plates. The width of leads varies from a couple of meters to over a kilometer. Leads can often branch or intersect, creating a complex network of linear features in the ice. In the winter, leads begin to freeze almost immediately from the cold air. —National Snow and Ice Data Center

Chapter 2

1. Defined in the Cambridge Dictionary as "a white layer of pieces of ice like needles that forms on objects outside when it's very cold." They can grow over an inch long overnight inside a tent in the Arctic.

2. A British explorer from the beginning of the 20th century; he was the leader of the ill-fated Endurance Expedition that was stranded in the southern polar region from January 19, 1915, to August 30, 1916. It has been called one of the greatest feats of survival in human history.

Chapter 3

1. "IPCC, 2013: Summary for Policymakers." Climate Change 2013: The Physical Science Basis. Contribution of Working Group I to the Fifth Assessment Report of the Intergovernmental Panel on Climate Change [Stocker, T. F., D. Qin, G.-K. Plattner, M. Tignor, S. K. Allen, J. Boschung, A. Nauels, Y. Xia, V. Bex and P. M. Midgley (eds.)]. Cambridge University Press.